MW01341169

The Power of CHRIST'S DELIVERANCE

The Power of CHRIST'S DELIVERANCE

EDITED BY

JAN J. MARTIN AND ALONZO L. GASKILL

Published by the Religious Studies Center, Brigham Young University, Provo, Utah, in cooperation with Deseret Book Company, Salt Lake City.

Visit us at rsc.byu.edu.

Printed in the United States of America by Sheridan Books, Inc.

Visit us at DeseretBook.com.

Cover and interior design by Emily V. Rogers

ISBN: 978-1-9503-0423-3

Library of Congress Cataloging-in-Publication Data

Names: Martin, Jan J., editor. | Gaskill, Alonzo L., editor. | BYU Easter Conference (2021 : Brigham Young University), author. | BYU Easter Conference (2022 : Online), author.
Title: The power of Christ's deliverance / edited by Jan Martin and Alonzo L. Gaskill.
Description: Provo, Utah : Religious Studies Center, Brigham Young University : Salt Lake City, Utah : Deseret Book, [2022] | Includes index. | Summary: "Because mortality is a test, we will all experience some dark days that may include grief, illness, disappointment, disillusionment, temptation, confusion, unanswered questions, and pain. The good news is that Jesus Christ promises deliverance from all of our mortal suffering and his promises are sure. While we wait for deliverance to come in his time and in his way, Christ's intimate understanding of our lives, our trials, our hopes, and our heartaches allows him to perfectly succor, strengthen, and refine us. Speaking from the annual Brigham Young University Easter Conferences in 2021 and 2022, authors Marie C. Hafen, Virginia Hinckley Pearce Cowley, Tyler J. Griffin, John Hilton III, Jan J. Martin, and Jennifer Reeder teach and testify of the power of Christ's deliverance"-- Provided by publisher.
Identifiers: LCCN 2021044280 | ISBN 9781950304233 (hardcover)
Subjects: LCSH: Jesus Christ--Mormon interpretations--Congresses. | Jesus Christ--Resurrection--Congresses.
Classification: LCC BX8643.J4 B97 2022 | DDC 232--dc23/eng/20211007
LC record available at https://lccn.loc.gov/2021044280

CONTENTS

INTRODUCTION

For most of us, the years 2020 and 2021 were unlike any that we have previously experienced. Unexpected and unwanted shelter-at-home orders, social distancing requirements, and mask mandates related to the COVID-19 pandemic sharply curtailed our customary lifestyles and helped create a widespread feeling of being endlessly entombed by circumstances beyond our control. Speaking in the opening session of the April 2020 general conference, President Russell M. Nelson acknowledged the uncomfortable restrictions related to the virus but also recognized that "life's personal trials stretch far beyond [the] pandemic." Current and future trials could be the result of "an accident, a natural disaster, or an unexpected personal heartache."[1] Because there have been, are, and will be days where "we have special need of heaven's help" and because we "need to be able to look forward to some respite, to something pleasant and renewing and hopeful, whether that blessing be near at hand or still some distance ahead,"[2] this volume includes essays that focus on the power of Jesus Christ's deliverance. In their different ways, each author invites us to "hope for our deliverance" in Christ (Alma 58:11).

In Hebrew, *Yeshua* (or *Jesus* in Greek) means "savior" or "deliverer." The English word *Messiah* originates from the Hebrew *Meshiach*, meaning "anointed." The Greek equivalent for *Messiah* is *Christos*, and it too means "one who is anointed of God." When these names are combined, the term *Jesus Christ* means "an anointed deliverer," an identity he boldly claimed at the start of his formal ministry. Teaching from an Isaiah scroll in a synagogue in Galilee, Jesus declared, "The Spirit of the Lord is upon me, because he hath anointed me to preach the gospel to the poor; he hath sent me to heal the brokenhearted, to preach deliverance to the captives, and recovering of sight to the blind, to set at liberty them that are bruised, to preach the acceptable year of the Lord" (Luke 4:18–19), and then said, "This day is this scripture fulfilled in your ears" (Luke 4:21).[3] As the Great Deliverer, Jesus can rescue us from "everything that threatens to diminish or destroy" our lives or our joy.[4] Sometimes his deliverance takes longer than we would like, but for those who put their trust in him, Christ's promises of deliverance are sure (see Mosiah 24:16–17; 25:10; 27:16; 29:20).

In the first essay of this volume, Marie K. Hafen explores the question "When Does Easter Morning Come?" She uses specific anecdotes to illustrate how to turn to Christ, focus on hope, and gain power to remain afloat during dark or difficult times.

In the second essay, Virginia Hinckley Pearce Cowley testifies of the ways that the Easter story inspires her to celebrate life and to be confident that Christ's promises of deliverance will be fulfilled. Following Sister Cowley, Tyler J. Griffin discusses ten important moments in Christ's mortal experience that helped define his character and built his capacity to endure the agony of the infinite Atonement of Jesus Christ. He believes that knowing how Jesus lived for us can empower us to strive to live for him no matter what opposition we face. John Hilton III's essay describes the way Christ's Crucifixion is generally perceived by Latter-day Saints. He proposes four ways that we can more effectively study the Crucifixion in order to obtain strength during times of opposition. In the fifth essay, I address moments of disillusionment and show how the Easter story affirms that disillusionment is not a tragic end but an important beginning for those who will apply divinely inspired principles of recovery. The good news is that we can successfully close the gaps between our beliefs and the truth. And finally, Jennifer Reeder discusses many of the specific burdens of mortality, especially physical illness. She teaches and testifies of Christ and shows that because of his atoning sacrifice, there is no earthly sorrow that heaven cannot heal.[5]

It is my hope that the experience, wisdom, and testimonies of these authors will strengthen your resolve to remain faithfully committed to the Great Deliverer—no matter what your personal challenges may be—and that, like the Book of Mormon prophet Nephi, you will also be able to confidently and firmly declare "the Lord is able to deliver us" (1 Nephi 4:3).

Jan J. Martin
Provo, Utah

NOTES

Many thanks go to Hank Smith, Alonzo Gaskill, Jeanine Ehat, Devan Jensen, and many others who helped arrange and produce the Easter Conferences for 2021 and 2022. I also appreciate Emily V. Rogers for the beautiful design and Mikaela Wilkins for proofreading the book.

1. Russell M. Nelson, "Opening Message," *Ensign*, May 2020, 6.
2. Jeffrey R. Holland, "An High Priest of Good Things to Come," *Ensign*, November 1999, 36.
3. *Old Testament Student Manual: 1 Kings–Malachi* (Salt Lake City: The Church of Jesus Christ of Latter-day Saints, 2003), 67.
4. Kyle S. McKay, "The Immediate Goodness of God," *Ensign*, May 2019, 107.
5. Thomas Moore, "Come, Ye Disconsolate," *Sacred Songs* (1816).

WHEN DOES EASTER MORNING COME?

MARIE K. HAFEN

Marie K. Hafen is a coauthor with her husband, Bruce C. Hafen, of several books, including The Contrite Spirit *and, most recently,* Faith Is Not Blind.

I wish we could sit together and talk in person about our experiences with life and living the gospel. But, as I write, I can feel we're together in spirit, and I'm glad we can connect through these words. My hope in sharing these thoughts with you is to rekindle our hope.[1]

We are living through some pressurized, demanding, sometimes even dark days. Perhaps we could even say we feel entombed by our circumstances. As we look to the Easter story, we might find ourselves asking, when will the stone be rolled away for me, for us? When will deliverance come, and how? When will my Easter morning come?

Perhaps we each could be asked the same questions that were asked of Mary Magdalene on that first Easter morning so long ago: "Woman, why weepest thou? Whom seekest thou?" (John 20:15). Remembering what happened that morning for Mary—in the doorway of that tomb—can lift our eyes, revive our hearts, lighten our feet, and bring us back to life.

It was an early morning just after Passover in Jerusalem. Mary, perhaps unable to sleep, had come before dawn to the borrowed tomb where Christ had been laid three dark days before. Finding the stone rolled away and the tomb empty, she ran to find Peter and John who ran back to the tomb to take in what she had just told them (see John 20:1–2). "For as yet, they knew not the scripture, that he must rise again from the dead" (John 20:9). Having seen the empty tomb for themselves, Peter and John returned to "their own home" believing, but no doubt also bewildered (John 20:10).

Mary remained, weeping.

I can imagine that she was exhausted but trying to wrap her mind around what she was not seeing. Where was his body? Where had "they" taken him? Looking into the tomb, she was greeted, this time by two angels. Their question of her was compassionate: "Woman, why weepest thou?" (John 20:13). But it didn't seem to console her.

She turned away from them, perhaps simply from being overcome with grief, only to hear the same question asked again—this time from someone standing outside the tomb, someone she mistook to be the gardener.

"Woman," he asked, "why weepest thou? Whom seekest thou?"

"Sir," she replied, without lifting her eyes and perhaps while barely able to breathe, "tell me where thou hast laid him, and I will bear him away."

THE RESURRECTION, BY HARRY ANDERSON.

"Mary." (John 20:15–16).

She heard her name. She heard his voice speak her name. Could it be he?

Of this moment, I wonder if there are any words in any language that can adequately describe what Mary felt. This is the moment that God's children had been watching for since Father Adam and Mother Eve first learned that a Savior would be sent to redeem us from the Fall and restore our access to God (Moses 5:6–9). This is the moment upon which all our hopes rest—when the victory over the grave was claimed and the possibility of our becoming one with God was affirmed. And yet, in all its universal and infinite significance, this moment was simple and intimate for Mary alone.

"Rabboni," she exclaimed (John 20:16).

The records say nothing of it, but can there be any wonder that she would have reached for him, that he would have reached for her? Whatever was unspoken between them privately, John recorded what Jesus did say: "Hold me not" (JST John 20:17), meaning, perhaps, don't try to keep me here, "for I am not yet ascended to my Father." But I have something I need you to do: "go to my brethren, and say unto them, I ascend unto my Father, and your Father; and to my God, and your God" (John 20:17).

He was saying to her, go and deliver the news to my brethren and, in essence, through them, to all the world that the plan of redemption is complete, the way for deliverance is prepared. To all generations he was proclaiming—by revealing himself to one—that the victory over death had been won.

Mary *heard* him, recognized and *turned* to him, then went and *did* what he asked her to do (see John 20:14–18).

In a broad sense, Mary's moment at the tomb—with her Master and our Master—marks the middle of what we have come to call the Easter story. The scope of this story includes each of us and stretches from our first mortal parents in the Garden of Eden through to our personal moments of return to our Heavenly Parents. How does this story go for each of us? for me, for you? Do we hear him, recognize and turn to him, and do what he asks?

Mary knelt, on each of our behalf, as it were, in the doorway of the tomb that could not hold the remains of God the Father's ultimate offering—his Lamb, his Son—placed on the altar of sacrifice for our sakes. Adam and Eve also knelt for our sakes in the doorway of time at the first altar of sacrifice. At the beginning of the Easter story, they didn't yet understand what it meant to sacrifice the "firstlings of their flocks" (Moses 5:5).

"An unblemished lamb in similitude of the Lamb? What does it mean?" they would have asked (see Moses 5:5–7).

Whatever they didn't yet understand—or remember, for the veil had been drawn—the Father had promised, before they left Eden, that a Savior would be provided for them and for us. A Redeemer from their Fall. A Deliverer from our bondage. A Repairer of the breach between us and God (see Moses 5:9).

But for this story to be complete, in order to make our return, we have to hear, turn, and do. We can learn much of how this is done by looking closely at how Adam and Eve did it. Their story is our story. It is the story of receiving Christ's Atonement.

LEARNING FROM ADAM AND EVE

Few artists have captured the depth of meaning in the Adam and Eve story quite as beautifully as Walter Rane. In his 2013 painting, *The Angel with Adam and Eve*, Rane focuses on the crucial

THE ANGEL WITH ADAM AND EVE, BY WALTER RANE.

moment when our first parents are introduced by an angel to how they—and their children—can return to the presence of God. As they kneel at their altar, they begin the story of salvation, of redemption, of deliverance. It is the beginning of the Easter story.

"Why," the angel asks, "dost thou offer sacrifices unto the Lord?"

"I know not," Adam replies, "save the Lord commanded me" (Moses 5:6).

The angel explains, "This thing is a similitude [or a likeness] of the sacrifice of the Only Begotten of the Father. . . . Wherefore, . . . thou shalt repent and call upon God in the name of the Son forevermore" (Moses 5:7–8). In other words, the heavenly messenger is teaching us, through Adam and Eve, to turn from our ways and follow the Son, even taking upon ourselves his name, in living the ways of God.

Rane's painting gives the angel a compassionate face. He, the angel, wants Adam and Eve to understand what he is teaching and to have a desire to do what they will need to do to ascend into the presence of God. He wants them to make the climb, to get themselves out of the mud of the world (in the lower right corner of the painting) and up into the light of heaven (in the upper left corner). The angel's radiance and posture draw the viewer's eye along a path that crosses directly over the sacrificial offering lying on the altar.

Adam and Eve aren't fearful. Rather, Rane shows them leaning forward, wanting to understand. Eve's hand on Adam's shoulder seems to be saying, "We're going to do this together."

In the Book of Moses, the Holy Ghost enters this scene and witnesses to Adam of the great plan of redemption (see

Moses 5:9), a teaching that fills Eve with illuminating insight. She and Adam have long since outgrown the innocence of Eden. By the time they are at this altar with the angel they've had children and grandchildren (Moses 5:2–3) and, no doubt, many hard experiences. Yet Eve "heard all these things and was glad, saying: Were it not for our transgression we never should have had seed, and never should have known good and evil, and the joy of our redemption." She's saying, "If we hadn't chosen to taste the bitter, we wouldn't—we couldn't—prize the good" (Moses 5:11). Lehi echoes these truths: no experience, no children, no misery, no sin—and therefore, no joy (see 2 Nephi 2:23–25).

Eve concludes, without the anguish "we" wouldn't know "the joy of our redemption, and the eternal life which God giveth unto all the obedient" (Moses 5:11). I love how she doesn't say "unto all the perfect," but "unto all the obedient"—those who are striving, sincerely trying.

The Book of Moses uniquely teaches that Christ and his atoning mission are central to the Adam and Eve family story from its earliest days through its last, and that mortal afflictions are designed not to punish but to teach us—by experience—to hear, turn, and do—how to become like God.

HEARING, TURNING, AND DOING IN OUR DAY

So how does what happened with Adam and Eve at the beginning of the Easter story help us as we live out our stories in these compressed, last days? How does what happened with Mary Magdalene at the empty tomb help us through our grief and bewilderment to still hear him, turn to him, and keep doing for him?

TRACY HAFEN

Tracy Hafen has some insights on this question; she shared this in a sacrament meeting talk recently:

> I can't comprehend all that God has in store for us. But I've had a taste of what it might be like.
>
> We have a daughter who had severe cerebral palsy. Her name is Chaya. One evening, a week before her sixteenth birthday, while Tom was out of town with a new job, Chaya passed away unexpectedly, without any signs or warning. The experience of her passing was actually beautiful, and I gathered with the kids in a circle around her and said a prayer of thanksgiving before the mortuary came to take her body.
>
> But after the kids were in bed, I felt a hole and a sadness that overwhelmed me. I threw myself on her bed to bury myself in her pillow and smell her face. I ached inside, wanting to hold her again. I thought about how the kids had been jumping on the trampoline after school that afternoon. I had felt too tired and busy to lift her from her wheelchair onto the trampoline, so I had just wheeled her over to watch the kids jump. I was filled with regret. But mostly it was a hole. Throughout the night, I cried, drifted off to sleep, woke to the gaping hole, over and over, wanting it all to not be true.
>
> The next morning, a couple from our ward who had lost a nine-year-old child in a bike accident many years earlier knocked on the door. I threw myself into Sister

Hendrickson's arms, sobbing, "How long will I feel like this? When will this hole go away?" For the rest of that day and into the next, I felt that hole. No matter what I did, it was there. And the regrets of everything I hadn't done with her that I felt I should have done surfaced over and over.

As I was reflecting on all the things I could have done better as a mom to Chaya, a voice came into my head: "I am not up here thinking about what you could have done better." With that thought, my mind immediately turned to our Heavenly Father's plan for us. I knew that plan. I had faith in that plan. In one moment—in that moment—the hole I had felt was filled with peace and even with joy.

A blanket of complete contentment settled over me. Though I had known the Spirit could bring comfort, I was astonished by this power. It was a palpable peace that I could not shake. It was as tenacious and ever-present as the hole had been the day before. This was the payment only my Heavenly Father could give, and I remember thinking at the time, "How can you do this? How can you make me feel like this?"

I said to Heavenly Father in my prayers that night that I would do anything, give up anything, sacrifice anything to have this feeling forever. If there was a being who could make me feel this way, I would do anything to be with that being forever.

Remarkably, this feeling remained with me to almost this same degree for several months. I remember thinking that God couldn't let this feeling stay forever, because I couldn't be tried or tempted when I was feeling like this. I couldn't get angry, I couldn't get impatient, I couldn't get

> discouraged. It was like heaven lived in my heart for a while, and I will never forget it.
>
> Those feelings of continual peace and joy gradually left me for the everyday ups and downs, but I have never had a moment of sadness about Chaya or felt that hole again. My sorrow was turned to eternal joy and an appreciation for the Atonement of Jesus Christ, that will allow us to be with our Father in Heaven, Chaya, and everyone we love for the eternities.[2]

Tracy *heard* forgiveness in Chaya's voice that brought with it a sweet reminder of Heavenly Father's eternal promises to us. Tracy *turned* from her regrets and allowed her faith in Christ's Atonement to fill the hole of sorrow she had been feeling with palpable peace. And that peace changes how she goes about the *doing* of her days.

ANN MEYERS ROMRIELL

My ministering sister, Ann Meyers Romriell, has this same kind of faith. Like Tracy's, it has been forged in life's fiery furnace. She has lost two dear husbands in untimely deaths, and now she faces her own from ALS. She recently wrote, "Yes, I am shocked and more than a little afraid for what will be ahead. Having said that. . . . I am feeling comfort and peace despite the inevitable. . . . I know that through the Atonement of Jesus Christ all will be made whole and that our mortal pains and suffering will one day be a distant memory."[3]

CAMARY WYNNE

Another dear friend, CaMary Wynne, also stricken with ALS, recently wrote this from a hospital bed set up for her in her bedroom, "My hands no longer work, and I'm typing with one (crooked) finger. Today I face death years before I thought possible. And I'm not afraid. . . . The Atonement is our foundation. It is our ticket home. Jesus Christ paid the way for each of us. But we have to do our part. We need not fear if we are living his commandments. I trust in him, and because of his Atonement my stupid mistakes are gone. And so long as I'm careful, the Lord will welcome me home."

CaMary is filled with this serenity and peace because she lived her life hearing him and doing for him. Over the years, every morning she has prayed, "What is most important for me to do today?" And, she says, "I have always received an answer."[4]

She and her husband, Lee, have helped many young people come to know what the Spirit of the Lord feels like by bringing them into their home, into their barn, or into their horse arena and teaching them how to build stable lives filled with the joy and peace of knowing and trusting God.

CaMary's body is declining rapidly, but her mind is active and eager. Now her challenge is to allow others to do for her what she would rather be doing for them.

CaMary and Lee inspire me to sift my thoughts and lift my faith when the pressure of life has me feeling beaten down and discouraged, when I am tempted to pull back, retreat, or shrink away from the demands of these intense days. Examples such as theirs, Ann's, Tracy's, Mother Eve's, and Mary

Magdalene's help me keep turning to him, listening for his reassurance, and doing for him.

Doing is powerful. Listen to what happened with a high-powered international executive from when he was a university student until now because he chose to do what was asked of him.

JEFF FRANKS

Jeff Franks, a graduate of Princeton, Harvard, and Oxford, has lived and worked all over the world in international economics and finance. He has served in the smallest of branches to the largest of wards. In an interview for a podcast recently, Jeff shared with me his experience in a tiny, limping branch from when he was a student at Oxford. He had increasingly felt like giving up on the Church—it just wasn't worth his time. Besides that he had some nagging unanswered questions about Church doctrine and history.

One Sunday he woke up saying to himself, "I'm going today, but I'm not going after this. . . . I'm not getting anything out of it. I don't fit in. They don't understand me."

That Sunday, wouldn't you know, the branch president "called me aside and asked me to be Primary teacher for a difficult set of ten-year-old boys. 'None of the women can control them,' he said. 'Could you do it? Could you try?' I was pretty hesitant, but I finally said, 'OK. I'll give it a try.'

"During the next year I came to fall in love with those little boys. I took them ice skating and to other activities. I had a chart. If they behaved they got a point. And if they had enough points, they got a treat." All of that "gave me a reason to go every Sunday. . . . I think I had some small impact on those boys, but they had a major impact on me."

He gradually discovered that "if you're not going [to Church] to *get* something, but you're going to *give* something, [that] changes your whole mentality about why we are there." So Church was no longer about his Church questions or "do I fit in" with the branch. Those kids and that calling changed not only Jeff's brilliant mind but also transformed his slightly hardening heart.

After that, "when tough intellectual questions would come up, I'd play a little game with myself: If I got to heaven and found out that my answer [to a particular question] was wrong, would it make any difference to me?" He decided it wouldn't, so long as he believed in and lived what he called "the core of the gospel," which "is in the first few temple recommend questions: Do you believe in God, Jesus Christ, and the Holy Ghost? Do you believe in Christ and his Atonement? Do you believe that the gospel has been restored? If you do, you're now asking about faith, repentance, baptism.

And now, "When I get to feeling pride sneaking in or a little ego, I think of my favorite Primary song, 'I'm trying to be like Jesus, I'm following in his ways. . . . Be gentle and loving . . . " Jeff quoted the entire verse and chorus from memory.

"I have a very strong feeling about my relationship with Jesus Christ. . . . And what I've learned over the years is, that's enough.

"I, too, can [now] attest that we receive the power of Christ's atonement as we 'try to love as He did in all that we do and say.'"[5]

As we listen for Christ's voice, how we do what he asks us to do is as important as the doing. Elder Maxwell taught that when we sacrifice the animal in us, when we place our broken hearts and contrite spirits on the altar, our doing shapes our becoming.

He put it this way: "If we are serious about our discipleship, Jesus will eventually request each of us to do those very things which are most difficult for us to do.[6]

No matter what we are asked to do, will we be . . .

1. Meek and humble instead of self-concerned, dismissive, proud, seeking ascendency?
2. Patient instead of hectic, hurried, or pushy?
3. Full of love instead of demanding, dominating, manipulative, condescending, or harsh?
4. Gentle instead of coarse, brusque, and vindictive?
5. Easily entreated instead of unapproachable, inaccessible, and nonlistening?
6. Long-suffering instead of impatient, disinterested, curt, and easily offended?
7. Submissive to God instead of resistant to the Spirit and life's lessons?
8. Temperate (self-restrained) instead of egotistic, eager for attention and recognition, or too talkative?
9. Merciful instead of judgmental and unforgiving?
10. Gracious instead of tactless, easily irritated, disingenuous?
11. Holy instead of worldly?

Such a list can make living the gospel feel out of reach. There are times when we all feel like shrinking, like pulling away from what we have been asked to do. In such dark days, we must remember that a Savior has been provided, that the angels will attend, and that we have each other.[7]

In the words of the Apostle Paul, we can cling to our faith "that the sufferings of this present time are not worthy to be compared with the glory which shall be revealed in us" (Romans 8:18).

In the words of our friend Thom Harrison, "These are difficult times. Times when our present pain is multiplied and enlarged. Times when we cannot in any way fight the enemy alone. Times where our combined faith in Christ holds us together moment by moment. Too great is the pain to ever endure it alone. Alone it will crush us. Alone we are destroyed by its accumulated strength. Yet together, . . . as a whole, with revelation, faith experience, testimony and the power of the Most High God, we gain power minute by minute. Not enough to destroy [evil] as yet, but enough to keep us strong, afloat, not conquered, not on our own, not defeated—strong enough to endure this time until we rise slowly towards the ultimate victory. Hold on, little flock. Our Shepherd is sure. Our Shepherd awaits us."[8]

Even Christ wondered if he had the strength to withstand the pressure that came with doing what he was asked of the Father to do (see Matthew 26:39, Luke 22:42). Even he had to stretch to his depths to avoid shrinking from his pain—from our pain (see Doctrine and Covenants 19:18). Even he leaned on the angels for support (see Luke 22:42). But he did not shrink! He finished the work he was given to do—work only

AN ANGEL COMFORTING JESUS, BY CARL BLOCH.

he could do (see Doctrine and Covenants 19:18–19). And because of him, the promise of deliverance from our tombs is sure!

What does it mean for us to "not shrink?" Staying open to learning from our experiences and staying supple to the Spirit, even when the supplications seem unheard for a time—perhaps a lifetime—is what it means to "not shrink." It is to stay trusting in his eventual deliverance of us even while our bitter cups seem bottomless and the chill of our winter seems endless. It is to be assured, no matter how dark the days and nights, that Easter morning is coming—for all of us!

NOTES

1. I am especially indebted to Martha Johnson for joining me in writing and editing this article.
2. Tom Hafen, email message to Marie Hafen, March 15, 2021.
3. Ann Meyers, email message to Bruce Hafen, December 11, 2020.
4. Personal conversations between CaMary Wynne and Marie Hafen, March to June 2021.
5. "Jeff: How a Harvard Graduate Found His Testimony in a Primary Classroom," *Faith Is Not Blind* (podcast), December 6, 2019.
6. Neal A. Maxwell in Bruce C. Hafen, *A Disciple's Life: The Biography of Neal A. Maxwell* (Salt Lake City: Deseret Book 2002), back cover jacket.
7. Neal A. Maxwell, "In Him All Things Hold Together" (Brigham Young University devotional address, March 31, 1991), speeches.byu.edu.
8. Thom Harrison, Facebook post, March 17, 2021.

CAUSE FOR CELEBRATION

VIRGINIA HINCKLEY PEARCE COWLEY

Virginia Hinckley Pearce Cowley is an author who served as first counselor in the Young Women General Presidency and on the Primary General Board.

I have no clear premonitions that my death is imminent. But I do know that at the age of seventy-seven I am walking through a veritable minefield. It seems that on either side of me at expected and unexpected moments, there is an explosion. Someone, a friend and contemporary, nearby, who felt mostly fine yesterday, has just received a diagnosis of inoperable cancer today. Or another simply does not wake up in the morning, having suffered a fatal heart attack or massive stroke. Or the multiple sclerosis or Parkinson's disease that has mostly been held at bay starts moving more rapidly and visibly toward its inevitable conclusion. I read the obituaries with one eye on the birth dates and the other looking for names I recognize.

But the ache I feel for those whose mortal life has come to an end and for we who love them is accompanied by a feeling of deep love and gratitude. Amid the ache of loss, there is additionally a feeling of elation. Here is someone who fought the good fight, finished the course, and kept the faith (see 2 Timothy 4:7). I want to jump in the air and high five each of them with a great big "You did it!"

At this Easter season, I wish to acknowledge my gratitude to the Lord by enumerating a few of the many things life has taught me—the truths that have piloted me through the storms and sunshine of life and that seem to shine more brightly every day—lighting the way to an unknown but gladly anticipated future. They are my reasons for celebration!

I celebrate the truth, the certainty, that the life he has given you and me is precious. My life is precious. Your life is precious. None of us know how long it will last, but we got to come! We got a body! No one else will have the same circumstances, the same innate characteristics and talents, the same stumbling blocks, the same opportunities. We are each wonderfully different. We are his work and his glory, and he wants us back (see Moses 1:39)! To that end, we are each given "one wild and precious life,"[1] and then we are given the power to choose what we will do with it. Life plus agency.

I love watching the two-year-old who has discovered the word "No!" He or she invokes its endlessly and loudly, reminding us how deeply is planted that desire to direct our own lives—to decide what and when. And then we get to learn from the consequences of our decisions. Honestly, that is cause for celebration. So now we are here—on this mortal stage, making decisions, responding to our weaknesses and our strengths and all the difficulties that are inherent in our mortal experience. Some afflictions we may have been born with, others we experience at the hands of others, and others come because of our own mistakes. But I stand here today to declare that God is a God of wonderful surprises. I celebrate the fact that he can take our afflictions and consecrate them to the welfare of our souls (see 2 Nephi 32:9).

Turning water to wine is certainly a miracle (see John 2:1–11), but in my life he has worked far greater miracles. With the Book of Mormon prophet Jacob, I know the greatness of God. He has consecrated—and I believe will continue to consecrate—my afflictions for my gain (see 2 Nephi 2:2–3). He has taken my troubles and turned them into wonder. He has taken the tragedies, large and small, and given me wisdom and compassion in return. Out of heartbreak, friends old and new have risen up to love me. Out of disappointment, new opportunities have presented themselves: "beauty for ashes, the oil of joy for mourning, the garment of praise for the spirit of heaviness" (see Isaiah 61:3).

The worldwide pandemic is certainly unique. When in the course of human history have so many on the planet experienced a common plague at the same point in time? But each of us experienced this affliction in a different way. What have been some of the wonderful surprises God has given you? How has he consecrated this particular affliction to the welfare of your soul? Has he sent beauty for ashes? The oil of joy for mourning? The garment of praise for the spirit of heaviness? If you don't see those compensatory blessings now, keep trusting and living righteously and I promise you miracles.[2] God has promised you miracles. Watch for them. Count them.

Now, a death and dying story—because I guess that's what you get from a woman with almost eight decades under her belt. Several years ago, I stood with a friend at the bedside of a man who knew that the end was near. He had suffered for more than a year with a terminal disease—no treatment and inevitable death. My friend held his hand and asked him, "What have you learned from all this?" It took him only a moment to make a short reply: "It's about relationships. Relationships are all that really matter." I was actually a little surprised at such a simple reply, but over the ensuing years I have continued to think about it. It makes sense to me to look at the whole of mortal life in terms of relationships.

Perhaps an axis is the way to picture it—a vertical line intersected by a horizontal line—a kind of plus sign. We could put my relationship with myself at the bottom, my relationship with the Father and the Son at the top, and on one end of the horizontal axis my relationship with family—on both sides of the veil. Then my relationship with community—my church community and all the humans in all spheres of my life—the human race—at the other end of the horizontal line. Let's talk about these four kinds of relationships one by one, understanding all the while that they are not discrete entities but are interwoven in organic ways.

RELATIONSHIP WITH SELF

First, my relationship with myself. Can I celebrate myself? How solid is my sense of intrinsic worth and identity? Do I really see myself as a child of God? One who carries his spiritual DNA and is loved and valued by him? This is critical knowledge, because I am the filter through which all my other relationships flow. I cannot hope to love, support, and celebrate others if I feel like a sham—an unworthy charlatan.

We get information about our worthiness from so many sources: our family of origin, others in our environment, life experiences. And building a healthy sense of self is not done in a day. It takes long and consistent effort. It takes picking ourselves up from the wounds inflicted by a world that has altogether too much meanness and criticism. It takes experiences that build within us a reservoir of strength and confidence. Experiences that teach us—that actually write upon our souls—that we have skills that enable us to engage with the world, making it a better place. Every time we solve a problem or learn how to do something, we gain confidence in ourselves and build that positive sense of identity.

RELATIONSHIP WITH THE DIVINE

But that's not enough. Our identity only becomes firm in the context of a real and constantly growing relationship with God the Father and his Son Jesus Christ. When we take our own given name and accept the gift of his name, we begin to glimpse the wonder of ourselves. The only 100 percent reliable source for this knowledge comes from our Father in Heaven. The kind of identity that really counts doesn't come from degrees or paychecks or numbers of clicks on our Facebook page. The way to have a relationship with the Savior—like anyone else—is to have more experiences with him.[3] That is frankly one of the best parts about having lived a lot of years—it is having had

MAN OF JOY, BY ANTHONY SWEAT.

so many experiences with the Lord that I have all but lost my fear of the future.

After the death of my husband, I remarried. Both of us were in our seventies at the time. We have been amazed at how joyful and easy our union has been. We believe that is somewhat because we both know who we are. Deep down. Because of our decades of experiences with the Savior in the past, we are deeply secure in our individual identity. Furthermore, we are sure that he will see us through—no matter what. As we strive to honor our covenants, he is bound to honor his promises to us.[4] President George Q. Cannon said,

> No matter how serious the trial, how deep the distress, how great the affliction, [God] will never desert us. He never has, and He never will. He cannot do it. It is not His character [to do so]. He is an unchangeable being; the same yesterday, the same today, and He will be the same throughout the eternal ages to come. We have found that God. We have made Him our friend, by obeying His Gospel; and He will stand by us. We may pass through the fiery furnace; we may pass through deep waters; but we shall not be consumed nor overwhelmed. We shall emerge from all these trials and difficulties the better and purer for them, if we only trust in our God and keep His commandments.[5]

Do you hear echoes of God's wonderful surprises? That he can turn every affliction to our gain? You and I can pray, asking God about ourselves.[6] Who am I? Do you really know and love me? We can then see that God communicates his unconditional and powerful love to us through the Holy Ghost, always available to you and me. We keep his commandments—because we love him, not so that he will love us!

Through priesthood authority we have been given the gift of the Holy Ghost. Paul tells us that the Spirit is like earnest money. Earnest money is a down payment that makes an agreement binding. So the presence of the Spirit in our lives is a down payment from God saying that he intends to have us live with him forever. And so our relationship with ourselves is most fully developed as we nourish our relationship with God!

RELATIONSHIPS WITH FAMILY

You can see how our axis begins to be circles overlaid on one another—my relationship with myself, my relationship with God, and now on to our other relationships. My life has taught me that our relationships with one another—family as well as the briefest encounter with a stranger—are the lifeblood of our mortality. They are cause for celebration. They give us a reason to get up in the morning. They fill us with purpose and with love.

Let's begin with family relationships. Wow! This is where there is so much joy—and so much heartache and pain. Our family relationships are complicated by our huge sense of responsibility—our hopes, dreams, and aspirations for our children in particular. But where else could we really learn about repentance, forgiveness, long-suffering, patience, diligence, faith, and tenacity? It's such an important laboratory precisely because we can never give up and we can always repent and do better. Elder Christofferson gives practical counsel:

> In reality, the best way to help those we love—the best way to love them—is to continue to put the Savior first. If we cast ourselves adrift from the Lord out of sympathy for loved

> ones who are suffering or distressed, then we lose the means by which we might have helped them. If however, we remain firmly rooted in faith in Christ, we are in a position both to receive and to offer divine help. If (or I should say when) the moment comes that a beloved family ember wants desperately to turn to the only true and lasting source of help, he or she will know whom to trust as a guide and a companion. In the meantime, with the gift of the Holy Spirit to guide, we can perform a steady ministry to lessen the pain of poor choices and bind up the wounds insofar as we are permitted. Otherwise, we serve neither those we love nor ourselves.[7]

But with the waiting and wanting there is still so much joy, so much day-to-day meaning through the companionship of others.

I love the reflective poetry in Ecclesiastes. In chapter 4 of Ecclesiastes, the writer describes our need for human connection: "Two are better than one; because they have a good reward for their labour. For if they fall, the one will lift up his fellow: but woe to him that is alone when he falleth; for he hath not another to help him up. Again, if two lie together, then they have heat: but how can one be warm alone?" (Ecclesiastes 4:9–11). That is a haunting question: "How can one be warm alone?"

RELATIONSHIPS WITH FELLOW TRAVELERS THROUGH LIFE

And yet in our world there are so many of our fellow travelers who are alone. "One study showed about 200,000 elderly people in the U.K. had not had a conversation with a friend or a relative in over a month. . . . Loneliness can kill. It's proven to be worse for health than smoking 15 cigarettes a day."[8] London is reportedly the loneliest city in the world.[9] In response to this very real health threat, the United Kingdom has formed the post of Minister of Loneliness. It is currently held by the Baroness Diana Barran. Germany and Japan also have high-level ministries tasked with ameliorating this epidemic. The data goes on and on. Japan is known to have cases of the elderly being found dead and alone in their homes sometimes months after the fact. Almost fifty million people in Europe don't meet friends or relatives at all throughout the year. They live in total isolation.[10] The poet's haunting question: How can one be warm alone?

Certainly, the coronavirus pandemic sharpened our awareness of loneliness. We knew that there were individuals in our families and neighborhoods who were isolated—day after day alone. We may have been one of those, but even if that wasn't our lot, we certainly found ourselves on our knees asking for ways to help those who were alone. More than half of adults in the Church today are widowed, divorced, or not yet married.[11] This does not mean they are isolated and lonely, but many struggle for a sense of belonging—a need for relationships.

And so, we recognize that on this axis or these overlaid circles, joy increases when our relationship with ourselves—our true identity—is understood through the power of our relationship with God. And when we love him and his Son, our love for our fellow men, including our family members, increases automatically. "A man filled with the love of God, is not content with blessing his family alone. [B]ut ranges through the world, anxious to bless the whole of the human family."[12]

Relationships with family members, with friends and neighbors, and with the perfect stranger allow us to grow and change. This life with all its people becomes a laboratory for becoming like him as we engage with others. Our bumping against people allows us to be damaged. And conversely, we will damage others. Our relationships sometimes create such discomfort that we are driven to our knees. Why else would we beg to forgive and be forgiven—to absorb pain and hurt and choose not to pass it on—to love as Christ loved—to become like him. Think about that. Could we really become like the Savior in the absence of our relationships with others? I think not. His central characteristic is love, and love requires the Other.

A CHURCH OF BELONGING

Standing on a lifetime of belonging, I celebrate my membership in The Church of Jesus Christ of Latter-day Saints. It affords me a covenant relationship with God—tying him, the sure keeper of promises, to me—with a clear path to follow, a keep-my-covenants path. My membership cradles me in a community, a community of believers who become part of my covenant responsibility and who are also bound by covenant to help and bless me. It's a laboratory where I can practice being a better human being: making mistakes, being forgiven and given the opportunity to try again. Yes, by covenant, it gives me the power (his power) to be better. It gives me an ever-growing number of individuals to learn from and to

IN REMEMBRANCE OF ME, BY WALTER RANE.

bless—an abundance of relationships! I love being a member of his Church!

At one time several of the beloved members of my ward were suffering. As a ward, we fasted, prayed, and wept with them. Our bishop reverently suggested that when we suffer with our brothers and sisters, in a very small way we are participating in the Atonement, where the Savior suffered for each of us. Since then, I have felt a sense of awe about my pleas and sorrow for individuals in my ward family.

And then there are the relationships beyond our families and wards. An abundance of our brothers and sisters on this planet to learn from and to love—whether it be the mechanic who fixes my car or the friend from second grade who suddenly appears at a reception or funeral or class reunion.

And so I celebrate relationships! All of them—with myself, with God, with my family, with my church family, and with every human who crosses my path! Certainly, one of the unheralded wonders of growing old is that every week—every single week—we bump into people we have known and loved on this planet. It may be in person or through a telephone call or a note, but it makes old age surprisingly delightful. Trust me, you're gonna love it!

THE POWER OF NATURE

Now, another reason to celebrate. I celebrate the life-affirming powers to be found in nature, recognizing that they are daily tangible evidence of God's love. Early-morning running or walking; hiking in the mountains; nurturing tomatoes in our backyard; heart-stopping sunsets; the technicolor wonder of flowers, butterflies, birds, water in every form—rolling waves, gushing streams, peaceful rivers, and the stillness of a deep clear lake.

You can tell
what's worth
a celebration
because
your heart will
POUND
and
you'll feel
like you're standing
on top of a mountain

and you'll
catch your breath
like you were
breathing
some new kind of air.[13]

Age pushes one to think about the prophets of old who recorded their last words to their posterity and people. I stand with them. At this Easter season in the winter of my life, I wish to declare my gratitude for mortal life—for agency; for the multitude of relationships I have been woven into; for the opportunity to seek after and experience his ever-constant love. I declare, first, last, and always, that I love the Savior. He is my King, my Redeemer. He is my greatest cause for celebration! With Nephi, "my heart groaneth because of my sins; nevertheless, I know in whom I have trusted. . . . O Lord, I have trusted in thee, and I will trust in thee forever (2 Nephi 4:19, 34).

That's all he asks—to trust him to bring us and those we love home to the Father again. To trust him to deliver on his promises. To trust his timing. To trust his perfect goodness. To trust his redeeming and constant love for me and for each of you.

NOTES

1. Mary Oliver, "The Summer Day," https://www.loc.gov/programs/poetry-and-literature/poet-laureate/poet-laureate-projects/poetry-180/all-poems/item/poetry-180-133/the-summer-day/.
2. Neil L. Andersen, "A Compensatory Spiritual Power for the Righteous" (Brigham Young University devotional address, August 18, 2015), speeches.byu.edu.
3. Neal A. Maxwell said, "Since experiential learning is etched deeply into our souls it is not easily forgotten." Neal A. Maxwell, *Not My Will, But Thine* (Salt Lake City: Bookcraft, 1988), 98.
4. Jeffrey R. Holland taught, "Just because God is God, just because Christ is Christ, they cannot do other than care for us and bless us and help us if we will but come unto them, approaching their throne of grace in meekness and holiness of heart. They can't help but bless us. They have to. It is their nature." Jeffrey R. Holland, "Come unto Me" (Brigham Young University devotional address, March 2, 1997), speeches.byu.edu.
5. George Q. Cannon, "Remarks," *Deseret Evening News*, March 7, 1891, 4; quoted by Jeffrey R. Holland, "Come unto Me," *Ensign*, April 1998.
6. M. Russell Ballard, "Children of Heavenly Father" (Brigham Young University devotional address, March 3, 2020), speeches.byu.edu.
7. D. Todd Christofferson, "Finding Your Life," *Ensign*, March 2016.
8. Jason Daley, "The U.K. Now Has a 'Minister for Loneliness.' Here's Why It Matters," *Smithsonian Magazine*, January 19, 2018.
9. "6 Loneliest Cities in the US," *9Kilo*.
10. "Loneliness: What Does It Do to Us?," *Medisana Health Magazine*, December 22, 2020.
11. M. Russell Ballard, "Hope in Christ," *Liahona*, May 2021, 55.
12. Joseph Smith, "Letterbook 2," p. 191, The Joseph Smith Papers.
13. Baylor Byrd, *I'm in Charge of Celebrations* (New York: Aladdin, 1995), 4.

I KNOW THAT MY REDEEMER *LIVED*

TYLER J. GRIFFIN

Tyler J. Griffin (tyler_griffin@byu.edu) is a teaching professor of ancient scripture at Brigham Young University.

Spring is a wonderful time of year when we're given the opportunity to celebrate the most glorious event in the history of the world—the resurrection of the Lord Jesus Christ. I love the opening lines of our beloved hymn:

> I know that my Redeemer lives.
> What comfort this sweet sentence gives!
> He lives, he lives, who once was dead.
> He lives, my ever-living Head.[1]

I want to approach the subject of Easter from a slightly different angle. I want to alter one word in that song and explore the effects that follow. What happens when we change the word *lives* to *lived*—I know that my Redeemer *lived*. This adjustment could be interpreted in a few different ways. It could imply an exclusive focus on the precise moment of Jesus's resurrection two thousand years ago. Rather than focusing solely on that singular event of Easter morn, I want to begin by going further back in time to briefly explore small moments that helped define his character. By seeing how he *lived*, we will better understand how he was able to grow "from grace to grace" (Doctrine and Covenants 93:13), build his character, endure untold agony brought on by the infinite Atonement, and ultimately rise from the dead to live again. By temporarily shifting our focus from *lives* to *lived*, we will be able to see more clearly how everything Jesus did and said was focused on helping others and doing God's will. Ultimately, knowing how Jesus lived for *us* can empower us to strive to increasingly live for *him*.

TEMPTATIONS

I know that my Redeemer *lived* for us as he faced and overcame every temptation. Matthew chapter 4 reveals Jesus enduring three intense temptations directly from the devil. He did not allow himself to indulge to *any* degree in *any* kind of sin! He didn't leave any room for the temptations to take root in his soul (see Hebrews 4:15; John 17:17–19). He *lived* for us through those temptations and withstood them, thus making it so that he would be able to fulfill his role as our Savior and Redeemer when the greatest test and darkest temptations would descend upon him nearly three years later.

To better understand the depth and breadth of the temptations Jesus overcame throughout his life and especially during his Atonement,[2] let's look at how he himself describes the experience of facing the powers of hell. When addressing Joseph Smith in Liberty Jail, the Lord listed many terrible conditions a person may face in mortality, many of which are attested in his own life (see Doctrine and Covenants 122:5–7).[3] As a final exclamation mark to that awful list, he told the Prophet, "And above all, if the very jaws of hell shall gape open the mouth wide after thee, know thou, my son, that all these things shall give thee experience, and shall be for thy good" (Doctrine and Covenants 122:7). Truly, Jesus *lived* for us, even while "[descending] below them all" (Doctrine and Covenants 122:8) and facing the very jaws of hell (see Isaiah 50:6; 52:14; 53:3–5; Matthew 27:26–35, 45–46; and Luke 22:43–44). Because he perfectly overcame all temptations, we can call upon him for help when we experience our own battles with the adversary today (see Hebrews 4:14–16).

TEACHINGS

I know that my Redeemer *lived* for us by focusing his life on teaching and revealing truth. He did this in a variety of ways, both directly and indirectly. One example of this is found through a fascinating interchange with his Apostles at the Last Supper. Thomas asked the question, "Lord, we know not whither thou goest; and how can we know the way?" (John 14:5). Jesus's response revealed the connecting point between all his teachings and our own efforts at discipleship. He said, "I am the way, the truth, and the life: no man cometh unto the

Father, but by me" (John 14:6). He was helping them to see there is no secret passageway or back door into heaven. We can't get there just by doing good deeds alone. *He* is the one and only path, or way, to salvation; we must come unto Christ to become more like him and allow him to save us. The way he helps us come unto him is through following his teachings.

Truly, Jesus *lived* for us every time he revealed his own characteristics, perfections, and attributes through his teaching. He helps us see that his teachings were much more than wise sayings; if we appropriately apply them, his teachings can become character-building blueprints we can use to develop divine attributes in our own life, patterned after his perfection (see Moroni 7:48).

MIRACLES

I know that my Redeemer *lived* for us through performing miracles. He healed. He fed. He sustained. He calmed. He gave life to the dead and sight to the blind and a new lease on life for those who had leprosy or who were lame or halt or withered in any manner. He didn't perform these wonders in isolation. His miracles are instructive object lessons and extensions of his teaching. Not only do his miracles reveal his power in the lives of people two thousand years ago, but they also sharpen our vision to recognize similar healings and blessings in our lives today.

The idea that Jesus lived for us through performing miracles becomes an invitation for us to walk with him and strive to do similar things. We can all seek to find miracles, both large and small, that need to be performed for people who

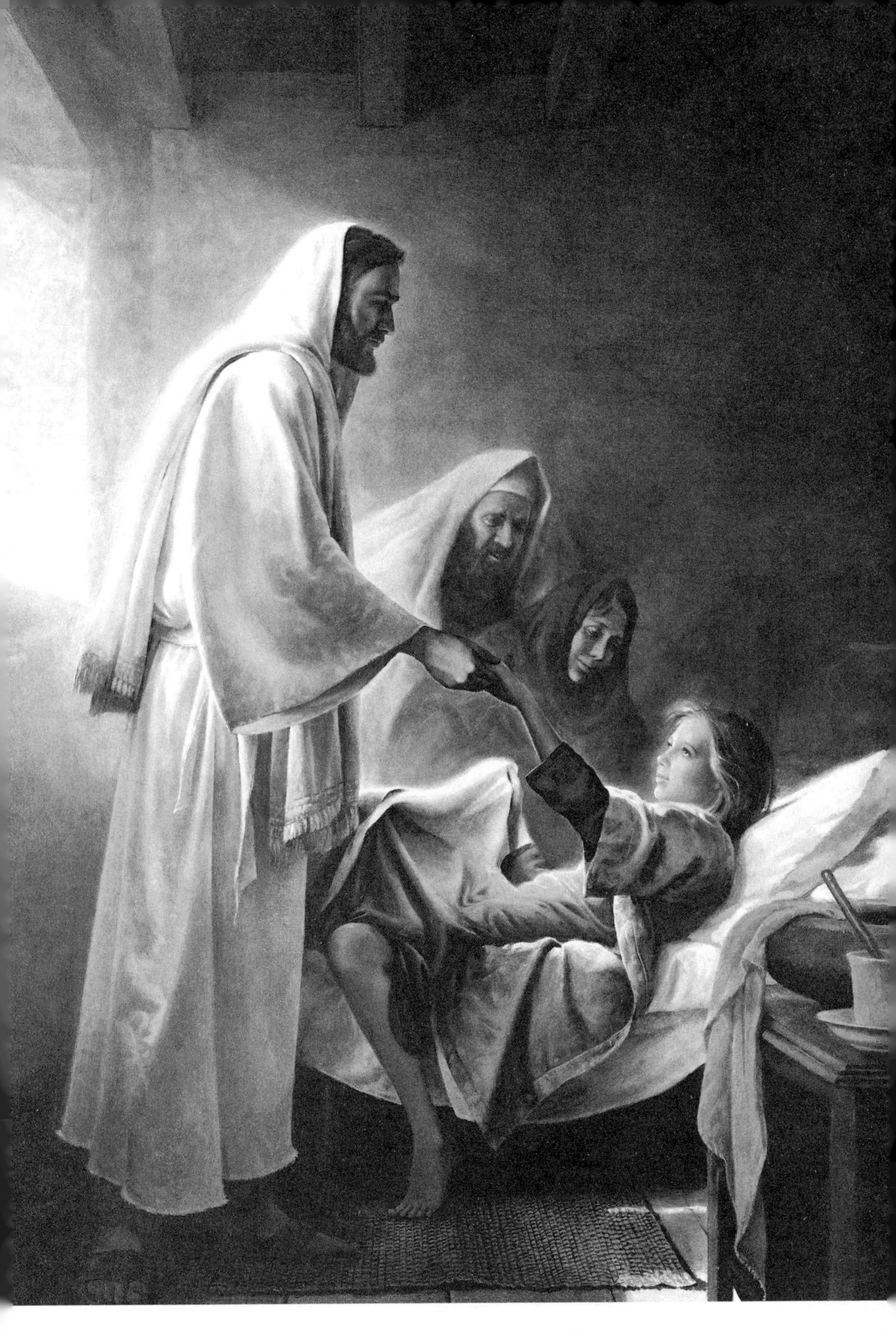

JESUS BLESSING JAIRUS'S DAUGHTER, BY GREG K. OLSEN.

are struggling all around us. This might be lifting up the hands that hang down or feeding the hungry or clothing the naked or giving powerful reassurance to people through blessings or prayer. It could be something as simple as taking the time to "mourn with those that mourn" or "comfort those that stand in need of comfort" (Mosiah 18:9) or to quietly sit with an individual who is struggling. His miraculous show of power and compassion among those who were suffering is another sign that he *lived* for us. It is also an invitation for us to strive to be a conduit through which heaven's power can also flow.

SERVICE

I know that my Redeemer *lived* for us through dozens of examples of selfless service when it would have been much easier and perfectly understandable for him to selfishly turn inward. An example of this selflessness is manifest when Jesus stood in the Kidron Valley, on Gethsemane's doorstep. On that night, after his Last Supper with the Apostles, he knew he was moments away from beginning the infinite atoning process. At such a crucial time, what could he say to his Apostles? John 14:27 gives us the answer: "Peace I leave with you, my peace I give unto you: not as the world giveth, give I unto you. Let not your heart be troubled, neither let it be afraid."

Jesus wasn't just going through the motions nor was he doing or saying things to get sympathy in return from his Apostles. Even at that moment, mere minutes away from infinite agony, Jesus resisted the natural human urge to turn inward, but instead turned outward with care and concern for those with infinitely smaller concerns than his own. Without providing great detail surrounding the infinite agonies he was about to face, he kept the focus on them. He knew how the events of the next few hours would leave the Apostles anxious and troubled, and he reassured them and offered them peace.

The Gospels give us many other examples of Jesus turning outward in the face of his own internal difficulties. For instance, when he received word that John the Baptist had been beheaded, Jesus "departed thence by ship into a desert place apart" (Matthew 14:13). The multitudes saw him leaving and followed on foot so that when he came to shore, there was a great multitude waiting for him. Instead of redirecting the ship, he came ashore and "was moved with compassion toward them, and he healed their sick" (Matthew 14:14). Amidst his own suffering on the cross, Jesus was concerned about forgiveness for his crucifiers (see Luke 23:34), consoling one of the malefactors hanging on an adjoining cross (see Luke 23:39–43), and assuring that his mother would be cared for by John (see John 19:26–27).

When we face major trials or difficulties, it is easy for us to become self-absorbed and overlook the needs of those around us. It is even harder to take the time to reach out in kindness and compassion as Jesus repeatedly demonstrated. Apparently, his command for us to "comfort those that stand in need of comfort" applies even in times of our own pain and extends to those whose needs and hurts might be less, and at times, significantly less, than our own.

GETHSEMANE

I know that my Redeemer *lived*, especially when it would have been much easier to die. He didn't just survive. He lived and thrived! Never was this reality more important than in Gethsemane and on Golgotha. As we pick up the story in Matthew 26:36, we're told that he came with them unto a place called Gethsemane, which means *oil press*. It's a place where olives were squeezed and pressed under tremendous pressure to get the precious oil out. What a beautifully symbolic name for what Jesus was about to do. Verse 37 tells us, "And he took with him Peter and the two sons of Zebedee, and began to be very sorrowful and very heavy." He turned to them and said, "My soul is exceeding sorrowful, even unto death: tarry ye here, and watch with me." Put another way, it seems he was expressing the feeling, "This is going to be much harder than I thought. I don't know if I am going to survive this ordeal in Gethsemane. Please stay awake with me." In the Doctrine and Covenants, he revealed more about the intensity of his suffering in Gethsemane by saying, "Which suffering caused myself, even God, the greatest of all, to tremble because of pain, and to bleed at every pore, and to suffer both body and spirit—and would that I might not drink the bitter cup and shrink" (Doctrine and Covenants 19:18).

As he went further into the garden, it appears that the awaiting burden came in infinite proportions, and it came quickly. After leaving Peter, James, and John, "he went a little further, and fell on his face, and prayed, saying, O my Father, if it be possible, let this cup pass from me: nevertheless not as I will, but as thou *wilt*" (Matthew 26:39). This is one of the most critical moments in all eternity for the Savior, as well as for us. As the initial pain and anguish of carrying our burdens came crushing down on him in that *oil press*, he fell to the ground on his face and pled with God to take it away.

Our physical bodies have natural aversions to pain, but this was pain beyond description; it was infinite agony. I can imagine that every element of his physical nature, everything he had inherited from his mortal mother, Mary, at that moment would have likely been pleading with him to give up the ghost and make it stop (see Doctrine and Covenants 19:15–19). I am so grateful that Jesus *lived* for us rather than giving up early or allowing his spirit to leave his body before the price of our salvation had been paid in full.

AGONY

I know that my Redeemer *lived* for us while enduring incalculable agonies throughout the atoning process. What was in Gethsemane's symbolic oil press so heavy that he fell to the ground on his face? We know from scripture that he is suffering for our sins, and sins have various consequences attached to them. When we break God's laws, we experience degrees of guilt, remorse, regret, shame, emptiness, and, at times, self-loathing. Jesus lived a sin-free life so he would have never experienced these negative feelings that come as a result of sinning. That all changed in infinite proportions as he suffered in Gethsemane.[4]

King Benjamin gave us the words of an angel who described the intensity of what Jesus endured: "And lo, he shall suffer . . . *even more than man can suffer, except it be unto death*; for behold,

GETHSEMANE, BY JORGE COCCO SANTÁNGELO.

blood cometh from every pore, so great shall be his anguish for the wickedness and the abominations of his people" (Mosiah 3:7, emphasis added). The pain and anguish he was enduring was clearly not something we can begin to comprehend. He couldn't let down his guard and give up. He didn't stop the process early, even though he had power to do so. His Atonement was a free-will offering, and he was using his agency to model for us what it means to endure to the end.

In addition to all the natural consequences for sin mentioned before, what else was included in the agonies of the Atonement? The Book of Mormon prophets give us additional insights to this question with statements such as "He suffereth the pains of all men, yea, the pains of every living creature, both men, women, and children, who belong to the family of Adam" (2 Nephi 9:21). King Benjamin said that in addition to our pains, "he shall suffer temptations, and pain of body, hunger, thirst, and fatigue, even more than man can suffer" (Mosiah 3:7). Alma the Younger added words like afflictions, temptations of every kind, sicknesses, infirmities, and death to our list of agonies (Alma 7:11–13).

Isaiah also added to our understanding of what Jesus experienced: "He is despised and rejected of men; a man of sorrows, and acquainted with grief: . . . he *was* wounded for our transgressions, *he was* bruised for our iniquities: . . . the LORD hath laid on him the iniquity of us all. He was oppressed, and he was afflicted" (Isaiah 53:3, 5–7).

By combining our biblical descriptions with those from the Book of Mormon, we see that Jesus's suffering included all mortal pain, anguish, illnesses, and infirmities whether they be physical, mental, emotional, psychological, or spiritual in nature. There is nothing we can teach him about disease, suffering, pain, abuse, heartache, or anguish that he doesn't already perfectly understand. Indeed, he is the only one who truly understands us. That understanding came at a terrible and infinite cost of his experiencing our struggles vicariously.

BETRAYAL AND ARREST

I know that my Redeemer *lived* for us in the face of betrayal and a threatening arresting party. After enduring his suffering in Gethsemane, the arresting party arrived in the garden in the middle of the night. It was Passover time, so there would have been a full moon overhead shining down on this group of men who had come with swords, staffs, lanterns, torches, and weapons (see Mark 14:43; Luke 22:52; John 18:3). Also bathed in that light stood Jesus, in quiet but powerful majesty, having just completed his suffering in Gethsemane.[5]

The power emanating from Jesus seemed to have a potent effect on the arresting party. In John's account, they seemed to be semiparalyzed in a moment of uncertainty after Judas had led them to the Lord. Jesus had to step forward and ask them, "Whom seek ye? They answered him, Jesus of Nazareth. Jesus saith unto them, I am *he*" (John 18:4–5). Notice how the *he* is italicized in the King James Version of this account. That means it was not present in the Greek manuscripts.[6] "I Am" in this verse came from the Greek words *ego eimi*. These are the same two words used in the Septuagint (Greek version of the Hebrew Old Testament) for the name of God in the burning bush while speaking with Moses.[7] In using these words, Jesus informed the arresting party that he was, in fact, the great "I Am" from the Old Testament, Jehovah, the God of Israel.

This bold declaration seems to cause the arresting party to fall backward to the ground (see John 18:6). Seeing no movement among the band of men, Jesus repeated the same question and gave the same response regarding his identity. In the face of Judas's betrayal and their attempts to arrest him, Jesus had the power to destroy all of them, but he didn't. Jacob, son of Lehi, gave us clarification on this and subsequent settings where Jesus could have easily defended himself: "it behooveth the great Creator that he suffereth himself to become subject unto man in the flesh, and die for all men, that all men might become subject unto him" (2 Nephi 9:5). Rather than fight back, he chose to submit willingly and meekly. In essence, he told these men, "Not my will, but yours be done."

At that point Peter came forward and cut off Malchus's ear.[8] Ironically, only one person came to Malchus's defense that night; it was the person Malchus had come to arrest. After telling Peter to put his sword away (see John 18:11), Jesus turned to the injured man. The Lord would have been completely justified in saying something like, "Do you really think that hurts?" Malchus was in infinitesimally less pain than that which the Savior had just endured in the garden. Rather than chiding, mocking, or ignoring Malchus's struggles, Jesus showed us what it looks like to "love your enemies, bless them that curse you, do good to them that hate you, and pray for them which despitefully use you, and persecute you" (Matthew 5:44). Jesus healed Malchus's ear (see Luke 22:50–51).

Many biblical scholars believe that the Gospels were written many years after the events transpired. This could explain why most of the miracles involve unnamed individuals;[9] their names were likely forgotten in the ensuing years. The fact that John gives us Malchus's name gives me hope that Jesus healed more than an ear that night. There are other possible explanations for why we know his name, but I have hope that something deep in Malchus's heart was also touched and healed. My hope is that he was later known as "Brother Malchus" by John and those who first received John's Gospel. Even if that didn't happen, I know that my Redeemer lived for us in showing us a perfect example in the face of betrayal, arrest, and evil opposition.

TRIALS BEFORE EARTHLY TRIBUNALS

I know that my Redeemer *lived* for us while facing judgment before the religious and political leaders of the people. Nephi summed up those trial experiences succinctly when he said, "And the world, because of their iniquity, shall judge him to be a thing of naught; wherefore, they scourge him, and he suffereth it; and they smite him, and he suffereth it. Yea, they spit upon him, and he suffereth it" (1 Nephi 19:9). Why would he suffer these things to happen when he had the power to stop the abuse at any moment? Nephi gives the answer at the end of verse 9: "because of his loving kindness and his long-suffering towards the children of men."

Once again, everything in his physical nature would have been pleading with him to give up or miraculously prevent the pain from being meted out by these people. To use Isaiah's phrase, "[He] gave [his] back to the smiters, and [his] cheeks to them that plucked off the hair" (Isaiah 50:6). He truly submitted and suffered all of the injustice and abuse. He lived for us so that he could ultimately fulfill the infinite Atonement on the cross.

CRUCIFIXION

I know that my Redeemer *lived* for us until he could say the full price had been paid. Shortly after being placed on the cruel cross, by soldiers who treated him with disdain and mocked him as the "King of the Jews,"[10] we hear the first of Jesus's final words: "Father, forgive them; for they know not what they do" (Luke 23:34). Jesus lived for us, even as he began the long painful journey on the cross that would lead to his death, by showing us an example of how to treat our enemies. He also showed compassion to a thief on one of the other crosses that day (see Luke 23:43) as well as his mother, Mary (see John 19:25–27).

Matthew informs us that from roughly noon to three p.m., darkness covered the land (see Matthew 27:45). During that time, the full weight of Gethsemane returned to him while hanging on the cross.[11] President Russell M. Nelson connected Gethsemane with Golgotha when he said,

> Under the direction of His Father, He was the creator of this and other worlds. He chose to submit to the will of His Father and do something for all of God's children that no one else could do! Condescending to come to earth as the Only Begotten of the Father in the flesh, He was brutally reviled, mocked, spit upon, and scourged. In the Garden of Gethsemane, our Savior took upon Himself *every* pain, *every* sin, and *all* of the anguish and sufferings *ever* experienced by you and me and by everyone who has ever lived or will ever live. Under the weight of that excruciating burden, He bled from every pore. *All of this suffering was intensified as He was cruelly crucified on Calvary's cross.*[12]

President Nelson was not the first to comment on the level of intensity of suffering on the cross. Elder James E. Talmage stated it this way: "It seems, that in addition to the fearful suffering incident to crucifixion, the agony of Gethsemane had recurred, intensified beyond human power to endure."[13] There are many possible reasons why Elder Talmage and President

Nelson would both describe the Savior's suffering as *intensified* from Gethsemane while on the cross. One factor here is the reality that there were no mocking crowds in the midst of Gethsemane's agonies like there were at Golgotha (see Matthew 27:42). Another factor could be Luke's Gospel describing an angel coming to strengthen him in the garden, but none is mentioned during his ordeal on the cross (see Luke 22:43).

Once again, every part of his mortal body would have been pleading with his spirit to give up the ghost, to not have to keep enduring this unfair and infinite agony. I stand all amazed at the love Jesus offered all of us by enduring those three hours, followed by asking for a drink and being offered vinegar (see John 19:28–30). What a glorious moment it must have been when he could finally say what have become three of my favorite words in all of scripture, "It is finished" (John 19:30). Only then could he freely and willingly give up the ghost. Only then did he allow his spirit to leave his body in the sweet release of death that finally stopped the infinite suffering, agony, and abuse. The price for our souls had been paid in full (see 1 Corinthians 6:20; 7:23). He had broken the bonds of hell and would soon break the bands of death through his resurrection (see 2 Nephi 9:7–12). His pierced body was quickly cleaned and hastily placed in the tomb where it would quietly rest for a short time.[14]

The timing is fascinating for the Jewish calendar that year. He died shortly before sundown on that Friday night. Once the sun set, it would have officially been the Sabbath day for the Jews, a day of rest. According to the Gospel of John, that particular Sabbath day was a high Sabbath because it was also the Passover celebration that evening.[15] The irony of this festival is that the firstborn of the Father didn't get passed over like all the firstborn who had been saved on the original Passover in Egypt, hundreds of years before. The blood of the lamb placed on the lintels of the door and the doorposts had preserved them from dying, but there was no salvation from death for the true Lamb of God on Calvary's hill.

RESURRECTION

I know that my Redeemer *lived* for us on that first Easter morning! It was a most triumphant day of eternity up to that point when Jesus broke the bands of death and walked out of the tomb, glorified and resurrected. From that moment forward, we could boldly declare our witness, "I know that my Redeemer *lives*!"

As we contemplate the story of Easter morning, I find it helpful to analyze how Jesus *lived* for us so to open the door for him to complete his infinite Atonement. Furthermore, it is helpful to analyze how I can seek to emulate his perfect example so we can symbolically live in him and he in us (see John 14:20). As we increasingly give our life to him as he completely gave his to the Father, he will increasingly guide, shape, polish, and protect us. His influence will continue to shape us as we face temptations, learn from and emulate his teachings and miracles, practice increasing selflessness, and endure our own agonies, betrayals, and trials of life. The fact that he perfectly *lived* for us allows us to now sing,

> He lives to silence all my fears.
> He lives to wipe away my tears.

RESURRECTION, BY JORGE COCCO SANTÁNGELO.

He lives to calm my troubled heart.
He lives all blessings to impart.[16]

Jesus didn't walk out of the tomb that morning just so that we could celebrate the event of his resurrection and leave it there. He rose from the dead so we could continually live as well—so we, through him, could have life in us. That life will continue to grow line upon line until that glorious day when, through him, we will ultimately overcome death and hell as well.

He lives! All glory to his name!
He lives, my Savior, still the same.
Oh, sweet the joy this sentence gives:
"I know that my Redeemer lives!"[17]

What joy it also brings to know that our Redeemer *lived* and that he will yet live inside each of us (see John 14:20) as we seek to allow him to touch our lives, to heal us, to bring life to those parts of our soul that feel dead, to bring new hope to those parts of our soul that feel blind or halt or maimed or leprous in any way. He promised, "I am the vine, ye are the branches: He that abideth in me, and I in him, the same bringeth forth much fruit: for without me ye can do nothing" (John 15:5). As we allow him to more fully become a part of our life, the reality that he *lived* for us will give greater meaning and depth to our declaration that he *lives* for us!

He lives, my kind, wise heav'nly Friend.
He lives and loves me [and you] to the end.[18]

NOTES

1. Samuel Medley, "I Know That My Redeemer Lives," *Hymns* (Salt Lake City: The Church of Jesus Christ of Latter-day Saints, 1985), no. 136.
2. Alma the Younger taught, "And he shall go forth, suffering pains and afflictions and temptations of every kind" (Alma 7:11).
3. The New Testament accounts attest to Jesus experiencing all the trials listed in Doctrine and Covenants 122:5–7 except those listed in verse 6 regarding being torn "from the society of thy father and mother and brethren and sisters; and if with a drawn sword thine enemies tear thee from the bosom of thy wife, and of thine offspring, and thine elder son, although but six years of age, shall cling to thy garments." His mission and travels did cause some rifts with some of his family (see Mark 3:21).
4. "It was required, indeed it was central to the significance of the Atonement, that this perfect Son who had never spoken ill nor done wrong nor touched an unclean thing had to know how the rest of humankind—us, all of us—would feel when we did commit such sins. For His Atonement to be infinite and eternal, He had to feel what it was like to die not only physically but spiritually, to sense what it was like to have the divine Spirit withdraw, leaving one feeling totally, abjectly, hopelessly alone." Jeffrey R. Holland, "None Were with Him," *Ensign*, May 2009, 88.
5. "The consistency of the Lord's willing submission and strong self-restraint is both awe-inspiring and instructive for us all. As an armed company of temple guardsmen and Roman soldiers arrived at Gethsemane to seize and arrest Jesus, Peter drew his sword and cut off the right ear of the high priest's servant. The Savior then touched the servant's ear and healed him. Please note that He reached out and blessed His potential captor using the same heavenly power that could have prevented Him from being captured and crucified." David A. Bednar, "Meek and Lowly of Heart," *Ensign*, May 2018, 33.

6. Italicized words are those added by the translators even though the equivalent word doesn't exist in the source texts written in the original languages of Greek (for the New Testament) and Hebrew (for the Old Testament).
7. See Exodus 3:14 where (ἐγώ εἰμι, *ego eimi*) is used where we read in English "I Am." John's gospel also emphasizes these two words, but they are especially powerful and relevant for this experience in Gethsemane as they were used in John 8:58.
8. See Mark 14:47; Matthew 26:51; Luke 22:50–51; and John 18:10–11. Note that all four Gospel writers included this story. We get Malchus's name only in John's Gospel. We only get a report of the miraculous healing in Luke's Gospel.
9. Most recipients of the Savior's miracles are described in generic terms such as the centurion's servant, the widow of Nain's son, ten lepers, a man born blind, a lame man who was at Bethesda, and so forth.
10. See Mark 15:2. Pilate referred to Jesus as the "King of the Jews" in all four Gospel accounts: Matthew 27:37; Mark 15:9; Luke 23:38; John 19:3. The only other time Jesus had been given that title was as a young child when the wise men visited him (Matthew 2:2).
11. "While he was hanging on the cross for another three hours, from noon to 3 p.m., all the infinite agonies and merciless pains of Gethsemane recurred." Bruce R. McConkie, "The Purifying Power of Gethsemane," *Ensign*, May 1985, 10.
12. Russell M. Nelson, "The Correct Name of the Church," *Ensign*, November 2018, 88; final emphasis added.
13. "In that bitterest hour the dying Christ was alone, alone in most terrible reality. That the supreme sacrifice of the Son might be consummated in all its fulness, the Father seems to have withdrawn the support of His immediate Presence, leaving to the Savior of men the glory of complete victory over the forces of sin and death. The cry from the cross, though

heard by all who were near, was understood by few." James E. Talmage, *Jesus the Christ*, 34th ed. (Salt Lake City: Deseret Book, 1962), 661.

14. We speak of his body being in the tomb for three days, but this was likely not a seventy-two-hour period. The Jewish day would have ended at sunset, shortly after they placed his body in the tomb (one or two hours at most). The twenty-four-hour Sabbath was followed by his being raised from the dead early in the morning of Sunday (less than twelve hours after sunset on Saturday). This would all add up to somewhere between thirty and forty hours in the tomb.
15. John speaks of the leaders of the Jews not wanting to enter the judgment hall of Pilate so they would remain clean for their feast that evening (see John 18:28).
16. Medley, "I Know That My Redeemer Lives."
17. Medley, "I Know That My Redeemer Lives."
18. Medley, "I Know That My Redeemer Lives."

THE LOVING CHRIST

JOHN HILTON III

John Hilton III is an associate professor of ancient scripture at Brigham Young University.

Let me begin with a simple question. How do you think the average member of The Church of Jesus Christ of Latter-day Saints would respond to the following statement: "Although Christ's Atonement was a process, where would you say Jesus *mostly* atoned for our sins? (a) In the Garden of Gethsemane. (b) On the cross at Calvary."

When some colleagues and I surveyed almost a thousand Latter-day Saint adults and asked them this question, 88 percent said, "in the Garden of Gethsemane" and 12 percent said, "on the cross at Calvary." One might think, "That is an unfair question—people were forced to choose between only two options." To remedy this situation, my colleagues and I asked 792 Latter-day Saint adults (who did *not* participate in the first survey) the same question and gave them a third possible response: "equally in Gethsemane and Calvary." But even with this third option, 58 percent—still a strong majority—selected Gethsemane only.[1]

This indicates a tendency among some Latter-day Saint adults to give priority to the atoning significance of Gethsemane over that of Calvary. In this essay, I will show how the scriptures, Joseph Smith, Church leaders collectively, the hymns, and the Savior himself more frequently talk about Christ's Crucifixion than they do his sufferings in Gethsemane. I will then provide two reasons why studying Christ's Crucifixion can help us and share two examples of how focusing on the Savior's sacrifice on Calvary can strengthen us spiritually. Before I continue, let me be clear that Gethsemane and Golgotha are both vital aspects of Christ's Atonement. They are not in competition with each other. My point is that some Latter-day Saints underemphasize the importance of Christ's Crucifixion. As we more fully embrace scriptural and prophetic teachings about the Savior's death, we will draw closer to him.

When I learned that Latter-day Saints heavily emphasized Gethsemane over Calvary, I was curious. Why was there so much emphasis on Gethsemane? Did it come from the scriptures? Across the standard works, there are two passages of scripture that talk about Jesus Christ suffering for our sins in Gethsemane.[2] In contrast, there are fifty-three passages that talk about Jesus Christ dying for our sins: twenty-one in the New Testament, eighteen in the Book of Mormon, twelve in the Doctrine and Covenants, and two in the Pearl of Great Price.[3] For example, at the beginning of the Book of Mormon,

THE CRUCIFIXION, BY HARRY ANDERSON.

Nephi recounts, "I, Nephi, saw that [Christ] was lifted up upon the cross and slain for the sins of the world" (1 Nephi 11:33).

The emphasis on Calvary also appears in the noncanonized writings and sermons of Joseph Smith, in which he only referred to Gethsemane one time. In this instance, he does not discuss its atoning significance; rather, he uses it as an example of Jesus doing the will of his Father. In contrast, Joseph Smith spoke or wrote about Christ's Crucifixion on thirty-four occasions. Nine of these are explicit statements that Jesus Christ was crucified for the sins of the world.[4] For example, in his 1832 account of the First Vision, Joseph wrote that Jesus said to him, "I am the Lord of glory. *I was crucified for the world,* that all those who believe on my name may have eternal life."[5] On another occasion, Joseph Smith said, "The fundamental principles of our religion are the testimony of the Apostles and Prophets, concerning Jesus Christ, *that He died*, was buried, and rose again the third day, and ascended into heaven; and all other things which pertain to our religion are only appendages to it."[6]

A focus on Calvary also exists when looking at the teachings of Church leaders from 1850 to the present. Collectively, for each one statement from Church leaders about Christ suffering for our sins, there are more than five about him dying for our sins. If we look only at the words of Church Presidents, the gap widens—for every one statement from a Church President about Christ suffering for our sins in Gethsemane, there are more than twelve about him dying for our sins on the cross.[7]

The hymns likewise share this emphasis. A study of four Latter-day Saint hymnbooks—the three earliest and the current one—shows that less than 1 percent of the hymns refer to Gethsemane, while 16 percent refer to Calvary.[8] For example, a popular sacrament hymn states, "We'll sing all hail to Jesus' name, / And praise and honor give / To him who bled on Calvary's hill / And died that we might live."[9]

To me, what is most significant is the Savior's own emphasis on his gift from Golgotha. In scripture, Christ personally refers to his experience in Gethsemane on one powerful occasion. In contrast, he refers to his death more than twenty times.[10] When Jesus Christ defines his gospel, his Crucifixion is front and center (see 3 Nephi 27:14).

Thus far, I have shown a juxtaposition between what the scriptures, Joseph Smith, later Church leaders, hymns, and the Savior himself have taught and emphasized as far as the atoning significance of Calvary relative to what the average Latter-day Saint adult seems to believe. Before continuing, let me be very clear—the events that took place in Gethsemane are a significant part of the Savior's Atonement; I am certainly *not* recommending we de-emphasize them. Many Latter-day Saints have focused primarily on Christ's sufferings in Gethsemane and not thought as often about his death on the cross. I'm not suggesting we reverse this error by exclusively prioritizing Golgotha and ignoring Gethsemane. Indeed, we should pay more attention to every facet of Christ's life, including his sermons, miracles, and actions.

At the same time, I have found that for many Latter-day Saints, an in-depth study of Christ's Crucifixion is particularly profitable because, in underestimating its significance, some of us have not studied it as carefully as we could. President James E. Faust taught, "Any increase in our understanding of

[Christ's] atoning sacrifice draws us closer to Him."[11] Better understanding *any* aspect of Christ's Atonement—including, and perhaps especially his Crucifixion—can deepen our relationship with the Savior.[12]

At this point, many readers are likely wondering, "If there has been such an emphasis on Christ's Crucifixion in the scriptures and elsewhere, why do so many Latter-day Saints seem to prioritize Gethsemane when it comes to the Savior atoning for our sins?" In trying to answer this question, incorrect speculations have been proposed. For example, some have suggested that Christ atoned for our sins and overcame spiritual death only in Gethsemane and then separately conquered physical death on the cross. Elder Gerald N. Lund called this a "doctrinal error" and wrote, "Nowhere in the scriptures do we find indications that the cross alone overcame physical death or that the Garden alone overcame spiritual death."[13]

A related doctrinal error comes if we minimize Christ's experience on the cross by saying, "What Christ experienced on the cross was no different than the suffering experienced by thousands of others who were crucified." That statement is false. The Savior's experience on the cross was completely different from other victims of crucifixion. Jesus did not just die—he "died *for our sins*" (1 Corinthians 15:3); his Crucifixion had atoning efficacy. President Russell M. Nelson taught that the suffering Christ experienced in Gethsemane was "intensified as He was cruelly crucified on Calvary's cross."[14]

Although the space available does not afford a complete answer as to why there is a disconnect between the beliefs of average Church members and collective Church teachings, possible reasons for an emphasis on Gethsemane by Church members include the following: (1) Latter-day Saints have a unique doctrinal understanding of the importance of Gethsemane and so have foregrounded it. (2) A handful of statements from Church leaders from several decades ago prioritized Gethsemane over Calvary. Some of these statements were published in past (but not current) Church curriculum materials, perhaps giving them outsized importance even though they are out of the mainstream of prophetic teachings.[15] (3) Perhaps the most significant reason Church members de-emphasize the atoning significance of Calvary is the lack of crucifixion artwork and cross iconography in our church buildings.

While not the focus of this essay, the scarcity of Crucifixion imagery merits attention. When Latter-day Saints are asked why their church does not display crosses, they tend to paraphrase words stated by President Gordon B. Hinckley in 1975. In response to a minister's question about the lack of a cross in a temple, President Hinckley responded, "I do not wish to give offense to any of my Christian brethren who use the cross on the steeples of their cathedrals and at the altars of their chapels, who wear it on their vestments, and imprint it on their books and other literature. *But for us, the cross is the symbol of the dying Christ, while our message is a declaration of the living Christ.* . . . The lives of our people must become the only meaningful expression of our faith and, in fact, therefore, the symbol of our worship."[16] It is important to note that in this same talk President Hinckley also referred to "the cross on which [Christ] hung and died," and said, "We cannot forget that. We must never forget it, for here our Savior, our Redeemer, the Son of God, gave Himself a vicarious sacrifice for each of us."[17] Thus, while de-emphasizing the Church's use of the cross as

1852 EUROPEAN EDITION OF THE DOCTRINE AND COVENANTS. PHOTO COURTESY OF MEGAN CUTLER. USED WITH PERMISSION; EDITION FOUND IN L. TOM PERRY SPECIAL COLLECTIONS, HAROLD B. LEE LIBRARY, BRIGHAM YOUNG UNIVERSITY, PROVO, UT.

an institutional symbol, President Hinckley emphasized the atoning significance of Calvary.

Symbols are multifaceted: they permit, even invite, layers of meaning. A cursory look at Church history indicates that the symbol of the cross has been viewed in different ways across the decades. For example, multiple nineteenth-century Latter-day Saints posed for formal photographs while wearing cross jewelry, including a wife and a daughter of Brigham Young. A cross appears on the 1852 European edition of the Doctrine and Covenants, and a floral cross was present at the funeral of John Taylor. In addition, a proposal for a cross to be placed on Ensign Peak was approved by President Joseph F. Smith, and a large cross is on the gravestone of Elder B. H. Roberts of the Seventy.[18] Consider a few quotes that illustrate the diversity with which the cross has been viewed by Latter-day Saints:

THE GRAVE OF B. H. ROBERTS.
COURTESY OF MEGAN CUTLER, USED WITH PERMISSION.

BRIGHAM YOUNG'S DAUGHTER, NABBY YOUNG CLAWSON (LEFT), AND HIS WIFE, AMELIA FOLSOM YOUNG, WEARING CROSSES.
© UTAH STATE HISTORICAL SOCIETY.

- Eliza R. Snow referred to "the triumphs of the cross."[19]

- A 1915 editorial published in the *Young Woman's Journal* stated, "The cross . . . has become a symbol of love and salvation."[20]

- A 1933 editorial in the *Relief Society Magazine* said that "Christ changed the cross into a symbol of Glory."[21]

- Elder Edward Dube referred to seeing an image of Christ's Crucifixion as one of the "defining moments" of his life.[22]

- Elder F. Enzio Busche said that looking at a crucifix helped him develop "a tremendous hope" in the redeeming power of Jesus Christ.[23]

Many similar examples could be provided. My point is that throughout the history of Christianity and even within the restored Church, faithful believers have had differing perspectives on how the cross should be used to represent Christ's atoning sacrifice. Regardless of how one views the cross as a symbol, we should focus on the doctrinal reality that Jesus Christ was, in his own words, "crucified for the sins of the world" (Doctrine and Covenants 53:2).

Thus far, I have demonstrated the scriptural emphasis on Christ's Crucifixion and provided a few possible reasons why church members have tended to focus more on Gethsemane. In the remainder of this essay, I will provide two reasons why studying Christ's Crucifixion can be beneficial and then share two examples of how focusing on Christ's Crucifixion can strengthen us spiritually.

REASON 1: CONNECTING WITH THE LOVING CHRIST

First, studying Christ's Crucifixion can help us connect with the loving Christ. Some Church members focus exclusively on the *living* Christ, and of course it is the living Christ that we worship. At the same time, we also worship a *loving* Christ, and the scriptures repeatedly teach that both Heavenly Father and Jesus Christ manifested their love for us through the Savior's death. For example, Paul declared, "*God commendeth his love toward us,* in that, while we were yet sinners, *Christ died for us*" (Romans 5:8; see also John 10:17; 1 John 3:16; 4:9–10). Jesus Christ himself called the Crucifixion his greatest act of love, saying, "Greater love hath no man than this, that a man lay down his life for his friends" (John 15:13, see also 2 Nephi 26:24; Ether 12:33).

Latter-day Saints throughout the decades have taught this same idea. For example, in 1910 Henry W. Naisbitt wrote, "When I think of the cross, the glorified cross, / On earth as in heaven above, / Resplendent forever undimmed it shall shine, / The eloquent symbol of love!"[24] In 1935 Grace Jacobsen poetically penned, "See the cross and bleeding feet . . . / Hear the message, tender sweet, / Hear him calling, gently calling / All mankind to Him above, / For He gave His life a ransom, / From the depths of perfect love."[25] Marguerite J. Griffin, writing in 1946, taught that Jesus offered his life "on the cross because of his great love for you and me."[26] More recently, Elder Dale G. Renlund stated, "Jesus Christ . . . loves and cares for us. He knows us and laid down His life for His sheep."[27]

Do you and I want to feel more love from Jesus?

Do you and I want to feel more love for Jesus?

Then let us study the Crucifixion—the event Christ personally defined as his greatest act of love. By better understanding the Savior's death, we will feel his love in greater abundance and be increasingly able to share that love with others.

Although we believe in the living Christ, we can also be strengthened by learning more about his sacrifice and death. Jennifer Lane, former dean of the faculty of Religious Education at BYU–Hawaii, wrote, "As we think about the Lamb slain from the foundation of the world, we can also know that he is the life and the light of the world: Christ as the sacrifice and Christ as the living Word. We don't have to pick which one to focus on because we can't have one without the other."[28] Jesus is both the living *and* the loving Christ.

REASON 2: BUILDING BRIDGES

A second reason to study Christ's Crucifixion is to remember that there are 2.3 billion Christians in the world and that nearly all of them believe Christ died for our sins, providing Latter-day Saints with a perfect opportunity to build on common beliefs. When I was a full-time missionary, if I saw somebody wearing a cross, I probably would have thought, "Oh, they are different." If I were a full-time missionary today, I would be so excited! I would say, "Hi, I can see from your jewelry that you probably believe in Jesus Christ. Could you tell me about your beliefs?" After listening, I might tell them about my beliefs or share a passage from the Book of Mormon that focuses on the importance of the cross, such as 3 Nephi 27:14.

Unfortunately, we don't always take advantage of opportunities to build on common beliefs. A Latter-day Saint woman who lived in the southern United States told me about inviting a neighbor to attend her daughter's baptism. When the neighbor presented the eight-year-old with a cross necklace, both the child and her mother froze, not knowing what to do. Sensing their discomfort, the neighbor took back the cross and said she would get the child a different gift. Regretfully looking back on this experience, the Latter-day Saint said that she wished she had seen this as an opportunity to rejoice with her friend in their shared belief in Jesus Christ rather than let it divide them.

Eric D. Huntsman, professor of ancient scripture at Brigham Young University, recounted the following:

> I remember being surprised once when a . . . Presbyterian friend corrected me when I told her that we preferred to worship a living rather than a dead Christ; she responded that she did too. The cross reminded Protestants that Jesus died for their sins, but it was empty because he was risen and was no longer there on it. I was chastened by her response, realizing that just as we do not appreciate others mischaracterizing our beliefs, neither should we presume to understand or misrepresent the beliefs and practices of others.[29]

Such mischaracterizations happen not only between Latter-day Saints and those of other denominations but also among Latter-day Saints themselves. A young adult told me that she had an institute sticker on her car that allowed her to park in the institute parking lot. She also had a cross hanging from her rearview mirror, which for her signified her belief in the Savior's Atonement. One day she found a note on her car that said, "Why do you have an institute sticker and cross on your car? Pick one!" I'm grateful this individual has remained firm in her commitment to the Church of Jesus Christ but wonder how many visitors or others have left because of unnecessary comments about the cross.

To be clear, I'm not suggesting we all start wearing cross jewelry. I am suggesting that you and I as individuals should let go of any stigma we feel about the cross, and we should certainly never put down somebody who wears or displays one. Let us celebrate those who believe in Jesus Christ and are willing to publicly proclaim their belief in him—however they manifest it. The doctrinal significance of Christ's Crucifixion is much more important than whether one uses a specific symbol. As we embrace and learn more about the Crucifixion of Jesus Christ, we will find that we have something in common with other Christians and a great opportunity to build bridges.

ILLUSTRATION #1: UNDERSTANDING CHRIST'S CRUCIFIXION CAN STRENGTHEN US TO CARRY OUR CROSSES

I now turn to two illustrations of spiritually strengthening insights we can gain as we study Christ's Crucifixion. First, understanding the Savior's death can help us press forward despite extreme difficulties. The book of Hebrews teaches,

"Jesus . . . for the joy that was set before him endured the cross, despising the shame, and is set down at the right hand of the throne of God" (Hebrews 12:2). Similarly, the Book of Mormon prophet Jacob spoke of those "who have endured the crosses of the world, and despised the shame of it, they shall inherit the kingdom of God, which was prepared for them from the foundation of the world, and their joy shall be full forever" (2 Nephi 9:18). Note that in both passages, there is a connection between enduring a cross, despising the shame of the cross, and finding joy.

As we follow the path of Christian discipleship, we will bear crosses and perhaps be shamed by others for our belief in Christ and his teachings. But Jesus endured his cross and received great joy; he says to each of us, "If any want to become my followers, let them deny themselves and take up their cross daily and follow me" (Luke 9:23 NRSV).[30] Note that we are instructed to take up our crosses *daily* and do so while *following* Jesus.

Today when we hear the phrase, "Take up the cross," we perhaps think metaphorically about carrying our different burdens. How would Christ's disciples have thought about this phrase? The Greek word translated as "cross" in Luke 9:23 is the same word used to describe Jesus on the physical cross where he was crucified (see Luke 23:26). The disciples had likely seen others literally take up their crosses on the way to execution. Is it possible that to Jesus's disciples the phrase "take up your cross" had a more graphic feel than it does to us today? Evangelical scholar Dr. D. A. Carson writes,

CHRIST IN THE LAND BOUNTIFUL, BY SIMON DEWEY.

> In the first century it was as culturally unthinkable to make jokes about crucifixion as it would be today to make jokes about Auschwitz. To carry your cross does not mean to move forward with courage despite the fact you lost your job or your spouse. It means you are under sentence of death; you are taking up the horizontal cross-member on your way to the place of crucifixion. You have abandoned all hope of life in this world. And then, Jesus says, and only then, are we ready to follow him.[31]

Contemplating the realities of Roman crucifixion can deepen our understanding of Christ's call to deny ourselves, take up our crosses daily, and follow him. If we consider this invitation in a first-century context, as suggested by Dr. Carson, the vivid connection between Christ's taking up his cross and our taking up our own can move us to greater courage when we face challenging circumstances. The Savior did not flinch from the cross he faced; rather, as Paul wrote, Jesus "emptied himself . . . and became obedient to the point of death—even death on a cross" (Philippians 2:7–8 NRSV; see also 2 Nephi 9:18). Pondering Christ on his cross can strengthen us to deny ourselves, despise the shame of the world, carry our crosses *daily*, and follow Jesus—even when we feel like giving up.

ILLUSTRATION #2: CRUCIFYING THE SIN WITHIN

A second illustration of a spiritually enriching insight related to Calvary is how Christ's Crucifixion can help us overcome sin. The Apostle Paul writes, "Those who belong to Christ Jesus have crucified the flesh with its passions and desires" (Galatians

5:24 NRSV). Thus, Paul uses crucifixion language to motivate us to destroy any remnants of evil lying within us. In effect, Paul encourages us to nail our sins to the cross of Jesus Christ and leave them with him on Calvary.[32]

In this same epistle, Paul writes, "I am crucified with Christ" (Galatians 2:20). This visceral image suggests that to follow Christ, we must follow him to the cross and spiritually crucify the natural man or woman in each of us. In fact, at the conclusion of Galatians, Paul writes, "In the cross of our Lord Jesus Christ, . . . the world is crucified unto me" (Galatians 6:14). Think about those words: *the world is crucified unto me.* Paul seems to suggest that because of Christ's Crucifixion, sin can become less appealing, eventually becoming dead to us. While such a state may not come immediately, it will come as we increasingly draw closer to Jesus and understand his atoning sacrifice (see Alma 13:12).

How can we crucify our lustful flesh and thus decrease our desire to sin? At least one approach is to accept the Savior's personal invitation to fix our eyes on his crucifixion wounds. The living Christ has said, "Behold [meaning "fix your eyes upon"[33]] the wounds which pierced my side, and also the prints of the nails in my hands and feet" (Doctrine and Covenants 6:37). The more we remember what he did for us, the more we will do what he asks of us. Perhaps this is why the Book of Mormon prophet Jacob wanted all to "view [Christ's] death" (Jacob 1:8), and Mormon encouraged his son to let the death of Christ rest in his mind forever (see Moroni 9:25). Accepting the scriptural invitations to "behold [Christ's] wounds," "view his death," and let Christ's death "rest in [our] mind[s] forever" can strengthen us to, in Paul's words, crucify "the flesh with its passions and desires" (Galatians 5:24 NRSV).

CONCLUSION

Although Latter-day Saints tend to give atoning priority to Gethsemane, the scriptures, Joseph Smith, Church leaders, the hymns, and Jesus Christ himself all more heavily emphasize Calvary. Throughout the history of The Church of Jesus Christ of Latter-day Saints, there has been a diversity of opinions about the meaning of the cross as a symbol. Many Latter-day Saints have viewed it as a symbol of love, glory, and triumph, perhaps suggesting that some of us today could reevaluate our current feelings toward the cross as a symbol.

We will fortify our relationship with the Savior as we focus on an event he often uses to identify himself. Our feelings for Jesus will grow as we recognize him as both the living and the loving Christ. We will feel a greater abundance of the Spirit as we rejoice with other Christians in our common belief that Christ died for our sins. A deeper understanding of Christ's Crucifixion will strengthen us in our trials and help us to nail our sins to his cross—and leave them there. These and many other powerful principles will distill in our souls as we, in the words of the Apostle Paul, "glory . . . in the cross" (Galatians 6:14). Studying Christ's death can change our lives.

Of course, the Savior's Crucifixion should not be the sole focus of our studies. His life and his parables, his resurrection and his miracles also merit a lifetime of careful examination. President Russell M. Nelson has promised, "The more we know about the Savior's ministry and mission—the more we understand His doctrine and what He did for us—the more we know that He can provide the power that we need for our lives."[34]

In Doctrine and Covenants 46, the Lord lists several spiritual gifts. The *very first gift listed* is to know through the Holy Ghost "that Jesus Christ is the Son of God, and that *he was crucified for the sins of the world*" (Doctrine and Covenants 46:13, emphasis added). This testimony is a spiritual gift each of us can receive and develop at increasingly deeper levels. President M. Russell Ballard taught that every member of the Church is entitled to and can "develop an apostolic-like relationship with the Lord."[35] Learning more about every aspect of Christ's life and atoning sacrifice will help us gain this witness.

My heart is filled with gratitude for the Savior. He is "Christ crucified," "the Lamb slain from the foundation of the world" (1 Corinthians 1:23; Revelation 13:8). He is the one who "liveth, and was dead; and . . . [is] alive for evermore" (Revelation 1:18). He is "our peace," "our passover," "our life," and "our Lord Jesus Christ" (Ephesians 2:14; 1 Corinthians 5:7; Colossians 3:3; Philippians 4:23). May we each strive to learn all we can about him—including the sacrifice he made on Calvary.

NOTES

Significant portions of this chapter are drawn from John Hilton III, *Considering the Cross: How Calvary Connects Us with Christ* (Salt Lake City: Deseret Book, 2021), used with permission.

1. John Hilton III, Anthony Sweat, and Joshua Stratford, "Latter-day Saints and Images of Christ's Crucifixion," *BYU Studies Quarterly* 60, no. 2 (2021): 49–70, available at http://johnhiltoniii.com/crucifixion.
2. See Mosiah 3:7; Doctrine and Covenants 19:16–19. Other verses, such as Isaiah 53:4 and Alma 7:11–13, may connect to the Garden of Gethsemane, but the verses themselves do not directly reference Christ's sufferings there. Luke 22:44 speaks of Christ's sweat being like great drops of blood; however, it does not attach atoning significance to this event.
3. See John 3:14–15; 12:32; Romans 5:6, 8, 10; 1 Corinthians 5:7; 15:3; 2 Corinthians 5:15; Galatians 3:13; Ephesians 2:16; Colossians 1:20, 21–22; 2:14; 1 Thessalonians 5:10; Hebrews 9:15, 26; 10:10, 12; 1 Peter 2:24; 3:18; Revelation 5:8–9, 1 Nephi 11:33; 2 Nephi 2:7–8; 9:5; 26:24; Mosiah 14:12, 15:7–9, 12; 18:2; Alma 21:9; 22:14; 30:26; 33:22; 34:15; Helaman 14:15–16; 3 Nephi 9:21–22; 11:14; 27:14; Ether 12:33; Doctrine and Covenants 18:11; 20:23–25; 21:9; 35:2; 45:2–5; 46:13; 53:2; 54:1; 76:41; 138:2, 35, 57; Moses 7:45–47, 55. For a discussion of these passages, see John Hilton III, "Teaching the Scriptural Emphasis on the Crucifixion," *Religious Educator* 20, no. 3 (2019): 132–53, available at http://johnhiltoniii.com/crucifixion.
4. For a comprehensive discussion of Joseph Smith's teachings regarding these topics, see John Hilton III, "The Teachings of Joseph Smith on Gethsemane and Jesus Christ's Crucifixion," in *How and What You Worship: Christology and Praxis in the Revelations of Joseph Smith*, ed. Rachel Cope, Carter Charles, and Jordan Watkins (Provo, UT: Religious Studies Center, Brigham Young University, 2020), 303–29.

5. "Circa Summer 1832 History," [1], The Joseph Smith Papers.
6. "*Elders' Journal*, July 1838," [44], The Joseph Smith Papers.
7. For an analysis of these references, see John Hilton III, Emily K. Hyde, and McKenna Grace Trussel, "The Teachings of Church Leaders Regarding the Crucifixion of Jesus Christ, 1852–2018," *BYU Studies Quarterly* 59, no. 1 (2020): 49–80, available at http://johnhiltoniii.com/crucifixion.
8. John Hilton III, Emily K. Hyde, and Megan Cutler, "An Atoning Priority in the Hymns of Calvary and Gethsemane," *Journal of Mormon History*, in press.
9. Richard Alldridge, "We'll Sing All Hail to Jesus' Name," *Hymns* (Salt Lake City: The Church of Jesus Christ of Latter-day Saints, 1985), no. 182.
10. In mortality, Christ referred to his death at least ten times: Matthew 16:21; 17:22; 20:18; 26:2; John 3:14; 8:28; 10:15, 17; 12:32; 15:13 (this list does not include references in Mark and Luke that parallel those given by Matthew). In addition, after his Crucifixion, he referred to his death at least eleven times: 3 Nephi 9:21–22; 11:14; 27:14; 28:6; Doctrine and Covenants 6:37; 27:2; 35:2; 45:4–5; 52; 53:2; 110:4.
11. James E. Faust, "The Atonement: Our Greatest Hope," *Ensign,* November 2001, 18.
12. A careful study of the Savior's Atonement is vital; as Elder Joseph B. Wirthlin explained, "No other doctrine will bring greater results in improving behavior and strengthening character than the doctrine of the Atonement of Jesus Christ." "You'll Grow into It," *New Era*, November 2000, 40. For a short but powerful exposition of the atoning significance of Christ's Crucifixion, see Gaye Strathearn, "The Crucifixion," in *New Testament History, Culture, and Society: A Background to the Texts of the New Testament*, ed. Lincoln Blumell (Provo, UT: Religious Studies Center, Brigham Young University, 2019), 353–71.
13. Gerald N. Lund, "The Fall of Man and His Redemption," in *The Book of Mormon: Second Nephi, The Doctrinal Structure*, ed. Monte S. Nyman and

Charles D. Tate Jr. (Provo, UT: Religious Studies Center, Brigham Young University, 1989), 94.

14. Russell M. Nelson, "The Correct Name of the Church," *Ensign*, November 2018, 88.
15. Here I am referring to statements that specifically put down Calvary relative to Gethsemane. See John Hilton III and Joshua P. Barringer, "The Use of Gethsemane by Church Leaders, 1859–2018," *BYU Studies Quarterly* 58, no. 4 (2019): 49–76, and John Hilton III, *Considering the Cross: How Calvary Connects Us with Christ* (Salt Lake City: Deseret Book, 2021), 96–100.
16. Gordon B. Hinckley, "The Symbol of Christ," *Ensign*, May 1975, 92, emphasis added. This talk was slightly modified to become a First Presidency message in the April 2005 *Ensign* and also appears in the March 1989, April 1990, and April 1994 editions of the *Liahona*. This phrase has been quoted more than twenty times in Church magazines, manuals, and other writings of Church leaders.
17. Hinckley, "Symbol of Christ," 93.
18. For an in-depth discussion of these and other indications that the cross was favorably viewed by some early Latter-day Saints, see Michael G. Reed, *Banishing the Cross: The Emergence of a Mormon Taboo* (Independence, MO: John Whitmer Books, 2012).
19. Eliza R. Snow, cited in "Lucy Mack Smith, History, 1845," 334, The Joseph Smith Papers.
20. "The Drawing Power of the Risen Redeemer," *Young Woman's Journal*, April 1915, 260.
21. "The Light of the World," *Relief Society Magazine*, April 1933, 235.
22. Edward Dube, "Gaining My Faith One Step at a Time," *New Era*, April 2020, 31.
23. F. Enzio Busche and Tracie A. Lamb, *Yearning for the Living God: Reflections from the Life of F. Enzio Busche* (Salt Lake City: Deseret Book, 2004), 52.

24. Henry W. Naisbitt, "'Twas Calvary's Cross," *Young Woman's Journal*, March 1910, 137.
25. Grace C. Jacobsen, "Gently Calling," *Relief Society Magazine*, August 1935, 528.
26. Marguerite J. Griffin, "Echoes of Hope," *Relief Society Magazine*, April 1946, 226.
27. Dale G. Renlund, "Our Good Shepherd," *Ensign*, May 2017, 32.
28. Jennifer C. Lane, *Finding Christ in the Covenant Path: Ancient Insights for Modern Life* (Provo, UT: Religious Studies Center, Brigham Young University, 2020), 148.
29. Eric D. Huntsman, "Preaching Jesus, and Him Crucified," in *His Majesty and Mission*, ed. Nicholas J. Frederick and Keith J. Wilson (Provo, UT: Religious Studies Center, Brigham Young University; Salt Lake City: Deseret Book, 2017), 73.
30. Christ invites his followers to take up their cross in Matthew 10:38; 16:24; Mark 8:34; 10:21; Luke 9:23; 14:27; 3 Nephi 12:30; Doctrine and Covenants 23:6; 56:2 112:14. In this chapter I occasionally use the NRSV because of its gender-inclusive and simpler language.
31. D. A. Carson, *Scandalous: The Cross and Resurrection of Jesus* (Wheaton, IL: Crossway, 2010), 25.
32. Elder D. Todd Christofferson taught, "If we are among the penitent, with His Atonement our sins are nailed to His cross, and 'with his stripes we are healed.'" "The Love of God," *Liahona*, November 2021.
33. *American Dictionary of the English Language* (Webster's 1828 dictionary), s.v. "behold."
34. Russell M. Nelson, "Drawing the Power of Jesus Christ into Our Lives," *Ensign*, May 2017, 39.
35. M. Russell Ballard, cited in "We Are Witnesses," *Ensign*, July 2019, 17.

THE RESURRECTION AND RECOVERING FROM DISILLUSIONMENT

JAN J. MARTIN

Jan J. Martin is an assistant professor of ancient scripture at Brigham Young University.

An anonymous tract, printed in London in the 1800s begins,

> Good Friday—How comes it that this one day in all the year should be called 'good?' We are not apt to mark the anniversaries of the deaths of our friends in this way—yet this day would not be observed at all, except it were in memory of the death of one Who was more than a friend to every one of us. . . . Without all doubt the death of Jesus Christ was the very best thing that ever happened for us. . . . The resurrection could not have happened had not the Lord Jesus first died.[1]

This author's positive perspective of death aligns well with teachings of modern prophets who have asserted that without death there is no "beginning of a new and wondrous existence."[2] President Russell M. Nelson explains that while living in premortality we "eagerly anticipated the possibility of coming to earth and obtaining a physical body." As excited as we were to arrive in mortality, we regarded "returning home as the best part of [the] long-awaited trip," even though that return required that we pass "through—and not around—the doors of death." Like Jesus Christ, "we were born to die," but, thanks to our Savior's atoning sacrifice, we die in order to live.[3] Because death opens the door to new opportunities, there is ultimately no tragedy in it.[4]

Building upon this positive perspective of physical death, I will focus my remarks on a less obvious but equally important type of death inherent in the Easter story: the death of illusions, assumptions, unrealistic expectations, and of simplistic or false beliefs that necessarily precede a rebirth of our understanding of truth. Today, some social scientists identify this type of death as disillusionment,[5] and I believe that in the same way that the Easter story testifies that physical death and physical resurrection are both positive parts of humankind's "universal heritage,"[6] it also affirms that disillusionment, or the process of "being freed from false beliefs or illusions,"[7] is both a merciful[8] and a necessary part of our mortal education. My message is that the Easter story is for all wounded souls who have discovered information about a loved one, or about the gospel, The Church of Jesus Christ of Latter-day Saints, its leaders, or its history that contradicts what they thought they knew and who are feeling disoriented, deceived, betrayed, or even tempted

FEED MY SHEEP, BY KAMILLE CORRY.

to abandon their membership in the Church.[9] The Easter story not only testifies of disillusionment's indispensable pervasiveness but also affirms that rather than being a tragic end, disillusionment is an important beginning for anyone who will patiently grieve and mourn over their losses, who will courageously choose for misconceptions to die and for truth to live, and who will seek to become engaged, intentional learners.[10] One of the most joyous messages of the Easter story is that we can successfully navigate the necessary, often painful and challenging process of closing gaps between our beliefs and the truth.[11]

DISILLUSIONMENT ABOUT THE MESSIAH

To appreciate how the Easter story addresses disillusionment, we must first carefully set the stage by applying counsel that President Brigham Young once gave. He said, "Do you read [the scriptures] as though you stood in the place of the men who wrote them? If you do not feel thus, it is your privilege to do so."[12] Therefore, please imagine yourself living in Judea at the time of Jesus's formal ministry. All around you, messianic expectations are high. People are actively looking for the "one special individual who would redeem Israel." According to one dominant messianic expectation supported in Jewish texts, *the* Messiah would "have dominion over all earthly kingdoms," he "would be worshipped by all people," he "would judge the wicked," "overthrow his enemies," and he "would establish an everlasting kingdom." More specifically, he would be a liberating Davidic king who would throw off the terrible yoke of Roman oppression and bondage.[13] Infused with these prevalent ideas, you have spent nearly three years diligently following a potential messianic candidate, a man named Jesus of Nazareth, and you are convinced that he is the one you've been looking for. In fact, Jesus has just triumphantly entered Jerusalem surrounded by multitudes crying, "Hosanna: Blessed is the King of Israel that cometh in the name of the Lord" (John 12:13) and "Hosanna to the Son of David" (Matthew 21:15). He has authoritatively cleansed the temple (see Matthew 21:12–13), confounded the scribes and Pharisees (see Matthew 21:23–46;

22–24), and pronounced judgments upon Jerusalem (see Matthew 23:37–39; Luke 23:28–31). From your perspective, these are undeniable signs that Jesus intends to be the new king of Israel.[14] All that he needs to do now is overthrow the hated Roman government and begin establishing his kingdom. Your enthusiasm and excitement are high as you impatiently but joyfully await the impending revolution.

However, these dreams and expectations are abruptly threatened. During the Passover feast in the upper room, Christ confusingly declares he is leaving, prophesying that his followers will "weep and lament" and be "sorrowful" for a time (John 16:16–20). After the meal, Judas, a friend, an Apostle, a man in Jesus's inner circle, arrives at the Garden of Gethsemane with a great multitude holding swords and staves. Jesus, the man you believe is *the* Messiah, is arrested and taken away for trial (see Matthew 26:46–56). Much to your bewilderment and dismay, Jesus says very little in defense of himself (see Matthew 26:57–68). He appears entirely powerless and does nothing to escape his captors. He is dragged from the Sanhedrin to Pilate, to Herod, and back again to Pilate for worldly judgment without ending the proceedings (see Matthew 27:1–26; Luke 23:1–25). You watch in horror as he is stripped of his clothes and scourged by Roman soldiers (see Matthew 27:27–31) with no hint of that power you have seen him use so many times before.

What is going on? You begin to doubt your past experiences with Jesus and start to question how he fulfilled your messianic expectations. Was his power real? Dazed, you stumble into "a great company of people" bewailing and lamenting as Jesus staggers from Jerusalem to Golgotha (Luke 23:27).

There he is nailed to a cross and crucified. Jesus, the man you believed was the long-awaited Messiah, dies right in front of your eyes (see Matthew 27:32–50). Instead of overthrowing Rome, Rome violently overthrows him. Suddenly, an earthquake rends the rocks around you (see Matthew 27:51), but it is hardly less devastating than the internal tremors that are ferociously shattering your hopes and dreams.[15] How can this be? Crucifixion and death were not part of messianic expectations.[16] Crucifixion was for rabble-rousing aspirants and impostors.

You can't accept what you are seeing. Because you "trusted that it had been he which should have redeemed Israel" (Luke 24:21), you are slowly consumed with an indescribable agony. You could have coped with the "death of a teacher, or even of a leader," but how do you resolve the problem of a "failed but still revered Messiah?"[17] In your desperation to make sense of the situation, you are gripped by sudden fears: what if Jesus was a grand deceiver, a deceiver of the worst sort imaginable, and what if you had been gullible enough to believe him?

As we momentarily withdraw from the darkness of a disciple's disillusionment, a darkness that includes both the pain and shock of losing the physical presence of Jesus, a man whom the disciples dearly loved and expected to continue associating with, and the loss of deeply cherished messianic expectations, expectations which largely made up the foundation of their belief in Christ, the crucial question is "How do you cope when you discover that something you believe is not true?" According to President Boyd K. Packer, the scriptures contain "principles of truth that will resolve every confusion and every problem and every dilemma that face the human family or any individual in it."[18] If President Packer is right, and I believe he is, the scriptures must include principles of truth that will help us cope with disillusionment. Beginning with one of the rare and precious descriptions of a disciple's emotional reaction to the events surrounding Jesus's crucifixion, I hope to demonstrate that we can find scriptural principles for successfully surviving disillusionment.

GRIEVING AND MOURNING

In John chapter 20, John wrote that on the "first day of the week," Mary Magdalene "stood without at the sepulchre

weeping" (John 20:1, 11). Though Mary's tears are easy to neglect, they can be interpreted as powerful representatives of two important processes associated with successful recovery from disillusionment: grief and mourning. Grief has been defined as "the sum total of what we think and feel inside when we experience a loss."[19] Though we often associate grief with the physical deaths of those we love, there are many types of loss that "can plunge us into the deep well of grief," including the loss of relationships or the loss of special objects, jobs, or treasured beliefs, expectations, or ideals.[20] Because the intensity of our grief reflects the degree to which our emotional lives were intertwined with the object of our loss, "the more profound the loss, the more profound the grief will be."[21]

This is one reason why devoted Latter-day Saints who discover information that contradicts what they thought they knew are often emotionally and spiritually incapacitated by the discovery. Such was the situation of the devoted Mary Magdalene. Even though the Gospels present very little detail about Mary's relationship with Christ, there are important indications that they had more than a superficial one. To begin with, Mary was one of several women who traveled with Jesus and supported him financially (see Luke 8:1–3). But her presence at the cross when Jesus died (see John 19:25), her presence at the tomb when Jesus's body was initially laid to rest (see Matthew 27:61; Mark 15:47), and her presence at the tomb the morning after the Sabbath (see Matthew 28:1; Mark 16:1–4; Luke 23:55) suggest that her relationship with Christ was profound and deeply personal.[22]

What specific messianic expectations she had for Christ are not clear, but her anticipation of finding Christ's body in the tomb so that she could continue the respectful burial process suggests that she didn't understand his teachings about his resurrection and may have misunderstood other things about his mortal mission. The incomprehensible and distressing disappearance of Christ's body (see John 20:2, 13) may have been the final shock in the rapid series of emotional blows inflicted upon Mary and the other disciples over the course of Christ's arrest, crucifixion, and death. Mary's tears demonstrate that she felt her losses keenly. Crying, "a phenomenon that is unique to humans," is a natural response to deep emotion, particularly to profound sadness and grief, but it is also one of the most common and obvious ways that people mourn.[23] Mourning "is the outward expression of our grief" and, "in a broad sense, includes whatever acts we engage in to help us express our grief."[24] Thus, not only do Mary's tears indicate that she was experiencing deep emotional pain; they were one of the ways she was mourning through her pain as she stood outside the tomb.

What is particularly instructive about Mary's experience begins after she looked inside the sepulchre and saw two angels sitting there. The angels asked Mary, "Woman, why weepest thou?" (John 20:13). Rather than being an impatient or indifferent directive for her to stop weeping, as many readers may naturally assume, this insightful, empathetic question served important healing purposes. First, the question allowed Mary to identify and express the true pain and very real sorrow that she felt from her "shattering experiences,"[25] experiences that seem to have converged with her very real concern over Christ's absent body. By asking "why," the angels gently and wisely invited Mary to give her sorrow words.[26]

Second, the angels' question allowed her to continue mourning. Mourning, described as "one of the deepest expressions of pure love,"[27] involves embracing the pain of loss, a process that often requires the sufferer to create a liminal space, or a suspension, void, or absence of belief. Liminal space is "sacred space where grievers can hurt and eventually find meaning" through an unpressured reconstruction of their beliefs.[28]

Mary's failure to immediately recognize Christ when he appeared (see John 20:14) suggests that she was in a liminal space where she could hurt but could not yet attach clear meaning to the events. When the resurrected Christ asked why Mary was weeping and wanted to know what she was looking for (see John 20:15), he continued the healing process the angels had started. Christ's questions were also invitations to name and express her pain and to continue mourning so that she could eventually progress to a place where she could attach meaning through reconstruction.[29] As the master healer, Christ knew that bringing a fragmented world back together takes time, loving companions, and individual humility.[30]

This beautiful portion of the Easter story illustrates two important principles about recovering from disillusionment. First, those who are disillusioned may need to grieve and mourn over their lost dreams, ideals, beliefs, or expectations in the same way that they would grieve and mourn over a lost loved one. Second, friends, family, and associates should be both wise enough and patient enough to allow, and assist, disillusioned individuals to do both.[31] Because grieving and mourning are both individual and lengthy processes, disillusioned individuals may experience a wide range of emotions, such as denial, anger, a desire to bargain, or even depression, before they reach a stage where they can accept their losses and begin reconstructing their beliefs. As our exploration of the Easter story will show, successful reconstruction begins by humbly allowing misconceptions to die and truth to live.[32]

CHOOSING WHICH BELIEFS DIE AND WHICH BELIEFS LIVE

The Gospels candidly portray the disciples of Christ as imperfect people who, despite associating closely with the Son of God, held a mixture of true and false beliefs. For example, even though Christ, the master teacher, repeatedly taught his disciples that he would be betrayed to the chief priests and scribes, that they would condemn him, that they would deliver him to the Gentiles to be mocked, scourged, and crucified, and that he would rise again the third day (see Matthew 16:21; 17:22–23; 20:17–19; 26:1–2; Mark 8:31; 9:31; 10:32–34), the disciples consistently resisted the news. Their responses range from outright rejection (see Matthew 16:22; Mark 8:32), to confused sorrow (see Matthew 17:23; John 12:16), to fearful silence (see Mark 9:32; Luke 9:43–45). It seems that a combination of cherished messianic expectations, cultural baggage, and previous experience[33] significantly influenced their opposition because "the simplest thing cannot be made clear to the most intelligent man if he is firmly persuaded that he knows already."[34] Thus, even though Jesus taught "that he was to be slain and then resurrected,"[35] his disciples "either could not or would not comprehend" what he was telling them.[36]

In stark contrast, the Savior's Intercessory Prayer indicates that the disciples had accepted some important truths. Offered the night before he was crucified on behalf of his disciples and all those who would believe in him because of their words (see John 17:9, 20), the Savior began the prayer by outlining the ultimate quest for of all of God's children:[37] to know "the only true God, and Jesus Christ, whom [God] hast sent" (John 17:3). Three times during the prayer, the Savior carefully described what his disciples knew. He said, "Now they have known that all things whatsoever thou hast given me are of thee" (John 17:7); they "have known surely that I came out from thee, and they have believed that thou didst send me" (John 17:8); "and these have known that thou hast sent me" (John 17:25). In other words, Christ's followers understood two important core doctrines,[38] they knew that Jesus was "the Christ, the Son of the living God" (Matthew 16:16) and that his teachings, and the miraculous works he did, came from God (see John 7:16; John 14:10).

Because we are also people who understand some truths and not others, this portion of the Easter story offers important lessons. First, as President Packer taught, it shouldn't be surprising that "at any given time, [we] may not understand one point of doctrine or another, [or] may have a misconception, or even believe something is true that in fact is false. There [should not be] much danger in that [because it] is an inevitable part of learning the gospel. No member of the Church should be embarrassed at the need to repent of a false notion he might have believed. Such ideas are corrected as one grows in light and knowledge."[39] Because the process of learning inevitably involves some unlearning, we could all truthfully state, "'It ain't my ignorance that done me up but what I know'd that wasn't so.'"[40] Pride, especially the pride that blames others for our misunderstandings,[41] can make it hard for us to admit that something we believe, expect, or assume is wrong.[42] But no matter why we are in error, and no matter how we discover that we are in error, we can only move forward successfully by humbly admitting the error and by meekly revising our understanding as we learn more.[43] As Jesus taught, it is the truth that makes us free (see John 8:32), but freedom comes only if we are willing to abandon misconceptions and embrace the truth.

CHRIST IN THE HOME OF MARY AND MARTHA, BY WALTER RANE.

Second, the Easter story demonstrates that the disciples "knew enough [truth] to continue on the path of discipleship," even when some things they thought were true turned out to be wrong.[44] Once again, the resurrected Savior's interaction with Mary Magdalene is informative. Christ's unexpected and miraculous physical appearance before her confirmed her belief that he was the son of God, but he gave additional verbal corroboration when he said, "I ascend unto my Father, and your Father; and to my God, and your God" (John 20:17). Though Mary may have misunderstood some parts of the Savior's mortal mission, Christ knew that she understood who he was. His presence and words were encouragements for her to stay true to that belief even as she discarded other misunderstandings.

Similarly, when Christ appeared and spoke to the eleven Apostles, he confirmed their faith in him by showing his wounds and proving to them that he was not a spirit (see Luke 24:37–43), but he also told them, "Peace be unto you: as my Father hath sent me, even so send I you" (John 20:21). Like Mary, the Apostles may not have grasped much about the Savior's atoning sacrifice, but Christ's physical presence and verbal declaration of who his father was confirmed that it was not their hope in his identity that needed to die, but their hopeful illusions about what he came to do. Similarly, it was not their belief in Christ's divine power that needed to perish, but what they thought Christ would do with that power—the image of Jesus wielding military might, of winning political battles, and of taking a revolutionary stand against their oppressors—that needed to expire.[45]

Even though the events of the Crucifixion were devastating and traumatic, they were also merciful in giving the disciples important opportunities to permanently discard misperceptions that had blocked them from receiving greater knowledge and to refocus their attention on confirmed truths that would help them work through the things that they didn't understand.[46] However, one of Peter's experiences with the resurrected Savior shows that if the disciples were going to completely heal and grow from disillusionment, they needed to be willing to become more engaged, intentional learners. Those empty spaces in their minds and hearts that were once filled with false beliefs needed to be actively filled with truth.

BECOMING ENGAGED LEARNERS

John is the only Gospel that records an important visit that the resurrected Christ made to Peter and six of his apostolic associates. According to Elder Jeffrey R. Holland, these seven men might have mistakenly thought that because Christ had successfully brought about salvation for himself and everyone else through his death and resurrection, his work was done. In their minds, there was nothing more to do but cherish their memories of the previous three years and joyfully return to their former lives.[47] Because Peter's mind was often liable to contraction,[48] rather than diligently seeking to figure out what the Savior meant when he told the Apostles a few days earlier that "repentance and remission of sins should be preached . . . among all nations, beginning at Jerusalem" (Luke 24:47), Peter mistakenly led his associates back to contentedly fishing on the Sea of Galilee (see John 21:1–3).[49] If we adopt Elder

Holland's interpretation of this story, the Savior's patient handling of the situation is insightful.

After meeting the seven Apostles on the lake's shore and providing them with a simple meal of bread and fish, Christ asked Peter three times, "Simon, son of Jonas, lovest thou me?" Each time, Peter answered, "Yea, Lord; thou knowest that I love thee." Jesus's response was always, "Feed my sheep" (John 21:15–17). In true master-teacher fashion, this important interchange gave Peter the opportunity to become a learner because it gave him no easy answers, only more questions, such as: Why does my love for the Savior matter? Who or what are Jesus's sheep? Where are Jesus's sheep? How are the sheep related to my love for the Savior? How do I feed the Savior's sheep?

Simply defined, a learner is someone who has unanswered questions and hopes to find the answers to them.[50] During Christ's ministry, Peter had occasionally posed valuable questions to Christ which allowed the Savior to give Peter and his associates important direct instruction (see Matthew 18:21; 19:27; Mark 13:3–4). However, at the Sea of Galilee, the Savior gave very little direct instruction, only enough to spark the type of questions[51] that would help Peter discover for himself what he should have been doing instead of going fishing. The Savior knew what Elder David A. Bednar once said: "Answer[s] given by another person usually [are] not remembered for very long, if remembered at all. But an answer . . . discover[ed] or obtain[ed] through the exercise of faith, typically, is retained for a lifetime."[52] Peter, the senior Apostle, needed to wrestle with the questions that came from his conversation with Christ so he could receive "additional light and knowledge by the power of the Holy Ghost,"[53] the principal way that he would continue his relationship with Christ after Christ's ascension.

Similarly, many of those who have experienced disillusionment will find that increased engagement in the learning process is an essential part of their recovery. Sometimes Latter-day Saints fall into extremes—either in passively expecting the Church or someone in the Church to tell them everything or in believing that there should be a simple and immediate answer for every question. Both positions inevitably lead to disillusioning experiences, what many call "faith crises," because they deny the spiritual, mental, and physical exertion that is required for the discovery of truth.[54] According to Elder Richard G. Scott, "Profound spiritual truth cannot simply be poured from one mind and heart to another. It takes faith and diligent effort. Precious truth comes a small piece at a time through faith, with great exertion, and at times wrenching struggles. The Lord intends it be that way so that we can mature and progress."[55] Peter's need to become a more fully engaged learner suggests that we are expected to become that type of learner, too. As we do, we can recover from disillusionment, but we can also reduce, or even prevent, some traumatic disillusionment experiences from happening in the future.

CONCLUSION

As we celebrate Easter, a time of "second chances, clean slates, and new beginnings,"[56] may we remember that this beautiful story affirms that we will all face moments of disillusionment. But may we also remember that the Easter story testifies that such moments can become precious new beginnings if we will patiently grieve and mourn over our lost beliefs, if we will bravely allow our misconceptions to die and the truth to live, and if we will seek to become engaged, intentional learners. Closing the gap between our beliefs and the truth, though painful and challenging, is part of our mortal experience, but it can be done successfully if we wisely look to our Savior's life and follow his teachings.

NOTES

1. Anonymous, *Is This Day 'Good' for Me? A Tract for Good Friday* (London: Society for Promoting Christian Knowledge, 1800).
2. Joseph B. Wirthlin, "Sunday Will Come," *Ensign*, November 2006, 30.
3. Russell M. Nelson, "Doors of Death," *Ensign*, May 1992, 72.
4. *Teachings of Presidents of the Church: Spencer W. Kimball* (Salt Lake City: The Church of Jesus Christ of Latter-day Saints, 2006), 18–19.
5. Paul J. Maher, Eric R. Igou, and Wijnand A. P. van Tilburg, "Disillusionment: A Prototype Analysis," *Cognition and Emotion* 34, no. 5 (2020): 956–57.
6. Thomas S. Monson, "I Know That My Redeemer Lives," *Ensign*, May 2007, 24.
7. Vocabulary.com, s.v. "disillusionment"; Bill Jacobs, "Religious Disillusionment," https://liferesource.org/portfolio-items/religious-disillusionment/.
8. Jill Carattini, "Burying Our Illusions," https://www.idisciple.org/post/burying-our-illusions.
9. Michael A. Goodman, "Become a Seeker: The Way, the Truth, and the Life" (BYU devotional address, July 12, 2016), speeches.byu.edu.
10. Three books that offer other helpful approaches to disillusionment and doubt are Patrick Mason, *Planted: Belief and Belonging in an Age of Doubt* (Provo, UT: Neal A. Maxwell Institute for Religious Scholarship; Salt Lake City: Deseret Book, 2015); Terryl Givens and Fiona Givens, *The Crucible of Doubt: Reflections on the Quest for Faith* (Salt Lake City: Deseret Book, 2014); Bruce C. Hafen and Marie K. Hafen, *Faith Is not Blind* (Salt Lake City: Deseret Book, 2018).
11. Lawrence E. Corbridge, "Stand Forever" (BYU devotional address, January 22, 2019), speeches.byu.edu.
12. Brigham Young, "Progress in Knowledge," in *Journal of Discourses* (London: Latter-day Saints' Book Depot, 1881), 7:333.

13. Trevan G. Hatch, "Messianism and Jewish Messiahs in the New Testament Period," in *New Testament: History, Culture, and Society*, ed. Lincoln H. Blumell (Provo, UT: Religious Studies Center, Brigham Young University; Salt Lake City: Deseret Book, 2019), 74–77.
14. Hatch, "Messianism," 82.
15. Vera Nazarian, *The Perpetual Calendar of Inspiration* (Highgate Center, VT: Norilana Books, 2010).
16. Hatch, "Messianism," 77–78.
17. N. T. Wright, *Jesus and the Victory of God* (Minneapolis: Fortress Press, 1996), 658.
18. Boyd K. Packer, "Teach the Scriptures" (address to religious educators, October 14, 1977), ChurchofJesusChrist.org.
19. Alan Wolfelt, *Reframing PTSD as Traumatic Grief: How Caregivers Can Companion Traumatized Grievers Through Catch-Up Mourning* (Fort Collins, CO: Companion Press: 2014).
20. Karla Helbert, "Is It Harder to Mourn an Actual Loss or Loss of an Ideal You Never Had?," *GoodTherapy Blog*, July 26, 2011.
21. Steven Eastmond, "The Healing Power of Grief," *Ensign*, January 2014, 63.
22. Margot Hovley, "Mary Magdalene—Tower of Strength," *Ensign*, June 2019, 58.
23. Leo Newhouse, "Is Crying Good for You?," *Harvard Health Blog*, March 1, 2021.
24. Helbert, "Is It Harder."
25. See Jeffrey R. Holland, "The Ministry of Reconciliation," *Ensign*, November 2018, 79.
26. See William Shakespeare, *Macbeth*, First Avenue Classics (Minneapolis: First Avenue Editions, 2014), act 4, scene 3.
27. Nelson, "Doors of Death," 72.
28. Wolfhelt, *Reframing PTSD*.

29. Reyna I. Aburto, "The Grave Has No Victory," *Liahona*, May 2021, 85; Rob Gardner, "Portraying the Savior in Music," in *All In: An LDS Living Podcast*, April 10, 2019, 41:00–46:00.
30. Wolfhelt, *Reframing PTSD*; Elaine S. Marshall, "Learning the Healer's Art" (BYU devotional address, October 8, 2002, *BYU Speeches*.
31. Scott Savage, "Straight Talk on Overcoming Disillusionment," November 22, 2018, *Scott Savage Live*.
32. Kimberly Holland, "What You Should Know About the Stages of Grief," *Healthline*, September 25, 2008.
33. A. LeGrand Richards, "What I Now Believe about a BYU Education That I Wish I Had Believed When I First Came" (BYU devotional address, January 14, 1997), speeches.byu.edu.
34. Leo Tolstoy, *The Kingdom of God Is Within You: Christianity Not as a Mystic Religion but as a New Theory of Life* (Waiheke Island: Floating Press, 2009).
35. J. Reuben Clark Jr., "Jesus: Our Risen Lord" (general conference address, April 1954), scriptures.byu.edu.
36. Jeffrey R. Holland, "The First Great Commandment," *Ensign*, November 2012, 83.
37. C. Scott Grow, "And This Is Life Eternal," *Ensign*, May 2017, 83.
38. Corbridge, "Stand Forever."
39. Boyd K. Packer, "From Such Turn Away," *Ensign*, May 1985, 35.
40. Hugh B. Brown, baccalaureate address, Utah State University, June 4, 1965.
41. Lynn G. Robbins, "100 Percent Responsible" (BYU devotional address, August 22, 2017), speeches.byu.edu.
42. Corbridge, "Stand Forever."
43. Richard L. Evans, "Should the Commandments Be Rewritten?," *Ensign*, December 1971, 58; Keith A. Erekson, "Understanding Church History by Study and Faith," *Ensign*, February 2017, 59.

44. Neil L. Andersen, "Faith Is Not by Chance, but by Choice," *Ensign*, November 2015, 66.
45. Carattini, "Burying Our Illusions."
46. Richard C. Edgley, "Faith—the Choice Is Yours," *Ensign*, November 2010, 31–33; Bruce C. Hafen and Marie K. Hafen, *Faith Is Not Blind*, 100.
47. Holland, "The First Great Commandment," 83.
48. Parley P. Pratt, "The First Principles of the Gospel," in *Journal of Discourses*, 9:204.
49. Robert D. Hales, "Being a More Christian Christian," *Ensign*, November 2012, 90.
50. Scott D. Whiting, "Deepening Discipleship" (BYU devotional address, December 8, 2020), speeches.byu.edu.
51. David A. Bednar, "Seek Learning by Faith," *Ensign*, September 2007, 63–64.
52. Bednar, "Seek Learning by Faith," 67.
53. See David A. Bednar, "The Hearts of the Children Shall Turn," *Ensign*, November 2011, 27; Sheri L. Dew, "Will You Engage in the Wrestle?" (BYU–Idaho devotional address, May 17, 2016).
54. See Bednar, "Seek Learning by Faith," 64, 67.
55. Richard G. Scott, "Acquiring Spiritual Knowledge," *Ensign*, November 1993, 88.
56. Russell M. Nelson, "This Easter, Find Peace in Jesus Christ," ChurchofJesusChrist.org, March 28, 2021.

HONORING MORTALITY

JENNIFER REEDER

Jennifer Reeder is a historian and writer and is currently the nineteenth-century women's history specialist at the Church History Department of The Church of Jesus Christ of Latter-day Saints.

In January of 2021, I was diagnosed with shingles. When I complained to a friend of the open sores on my face and near my eye, she suggested that I do some journaling on what it means to honor mortality. I admit that I laughed out loud. How did my searing pain through the nerves in my jaw and teeth or the impending danger to my optic nerve constitute honoring mortality? Shingles seemed to push me over the edge, on top of living alone and everything shut down due to Covid. The drops I put in my eyes mixed with my tears as I coped through my daily struggle.

Suddenly the past ten years weighed down on me. In 2010 I was diagnosed with leukemia and had two years of chemo to achieve remission. In 2013 I relapsed and needed a bone marrow transplant. In 2016 the leukemia came back, this time in lesions on my sternum, ribs, and spine, requiring targeted radiation and a second transplant. That effort was delayed with a severe bout of pneumonia, the source of which was finally discovered after a bronchoscopy, a lung biopsy, and three months on oxygen. Since then, due to side effects and a weakened immune system, I have worked through graft versus host disease, where my donor bone marrow has attacked my own body, interstitial lung disease (a chronic condition), cataracts, dry mouth, and dry eyes. I don't think I should be old enough for this kind of body! Scars, radiation tattoos, bouts of baldness, infertility, and now my second bout of shingles. How in the world am I supposed to honor mortality when some days I'm not even sure I want to wake up to this body? This is certainly the depths of mortality.

I resonate with Jane Snyder Richards's account. Her husband had been sent on a mission soon after the family fled Nauvoo in 1846. Her two-year-old daughter became ill, and Jane delivered a baby boy in her wagon, who died an hour after birth. Two months later, in September, her little girl grew worse. Jane wrote, "There was a time when I had thought she might live and then it seemed as though all I had suffered would seem but a dream." Unfortunately, the toddler died, and Jane continued her account: "Now she was taken my own life seemed only a burden. My Husband was to be away for two years and the hardships he might suffer made his return seem most uncertain." Jane was all alone in the middle of the mud and the inhumane conditions. I think she could hardly summon up her strength, because she wrote, "I only lived because I could not die."[1]

Have you ever felt the burden of mortality? Handcart pioneer Priscilla Evans wrote upon reaching the Salt Lake Valley in 1856, that she was "tired, sick foot sore and weary."[2] Both Melissa Morgan Dodge and Ann Marsh Abbott separately described at the end of some pretty extreme afflictions that they were now "in the land of the living."[3] The physical part of mortality is just so physical. Physical and mental health, disabilities, broken bodies, disease, virus, age—strangely, by design, all these things wear us down. I have had a lot of reactions to my physical trials: "Everything happens for a reason." "You should try a plant-based diet." "Maybe you needed a course correction." "This is part of Heavenly Father's plan for you." I reject these trite explanations. I believe that I chose to come to earth, to be born into an imperfect body in a fallen world with the possibility that my DNA might slip and produce lymphoblastic cells rather than regular blood cells. I also believe in the law of compensation, the gospel of restoration, the good news of Jesus Christ—that a way would open for me, whether that be through well-trained medical doctors and new drugs and technology or through fasting and prayers of my family, friends, and ward or through a combination of both faith and science. It is part of my mortal existence.

At this Easter season, we celebrate the good news of the gospel—the resurrection and redemption of Jesus Christ and his gift of salvation and exaltation offered to all of us. I believe the best way to understand this gift is to recognize its cost. I want to talk about what it means to honor mortality. I think we need to understand this time and recognize the physical, emotional, and social aspects that could be achieved only with a physical body, with its limits and far reaches, its sorrows and joys, and the promise of renewal, restoration, compensation, and hope.

There are some amazing things that we experience with our mortal bodies. I used to be a fit, healthy young woman who ran marathons and loved hiking, the gym, and physical activity. There is nothing like that finish-line energy spurt where your heart pumps and your blood flows and your muscles stretch as you suddenly find a very last bit of momentum to stretch across the finish line. Or when you finally reach the top of that never-ending mountain and gaze over a breathtaking view. Now my lungs and legs allow me to walk through my neighborhood or do yoga, where I engage deep breathing to establish core balance, then spread my limbs and my back in ways that invigorate me beyond my own capacity. Sight! Sound! Taste! Touch! Smells! All have so many incredible sensations. We can sing and dance; we travel and work and plant and reap. We are living the law of the harvest. Oh, it is so good to be alive!

And yet it's so hard. So much ugliness, chilling sounds, bitter tastes, abusive touch, and stench. Exhaustion, depression, addiction, so many emotions. Sometimes I wonder, knowing what I know now, if I really did shout for joy upon hearing about this mortal part of the plan (see Job 38:7). Or celebrate the courageous act of "our glorious mother Eve" in choosing the bitter fruit that would bring us here (see Doctrine and Covenants 138:39). I think to an extent, we all experience what she and Adam did: a creation, a Fall, a covenant, and time—time to learn how to fill the measure of our creation; to multiply and replenish and create good, beautiful things; to

wander through our own wildernesses and deal with the briars and noxious weeds.

Have you ever thought about the doctrinal aspect of the human body? The restored gospel reveals the need to perform proxy ordinances for the dead, those that do not have bodies, including baptism. Like Eve, those of us who have made sacred covenants in the temple know of the very physical blessings that come in the initiatory, that each part of our bodies can be made strong and holy. As an ordinance worker in the Salt Lake Temple before it closed, I grappled a lot with those promises, myself having an imperfect physical body, broken down by chemo and radiation and life. I realized that some of those promises are for here and now, like bearing the burdens I am called to bear. But some of these are for my future, like health in my navel, marrow to my bones, and running without weariness or walking without fainting (see Proverbs 3:8; Doctrine and Covenants 89:18, 20).

Take, for example, the way we learn about Christ. We know that he was born to "dwell in a tabernacle of clay," wherein he would suffer "pains and afflictions and temptations of every kind," and "the pains and the sicknesses of his people," including death, infirmities, and sins (Mosiah 3:5; Alma 7:11–13). When he was resurrected, he continued to bear the marks of the crucifixion. At a most sacred, intimate moment when he appeared on the American continent, he asked those who had survived earthquakes, mass destruction, and chaos to come thrust their hands into his side, to feel the nail prints in his hands and feet (see 3 Nephi 11:14; Mosiah 2:9). Two of my favorite hymns express that physicality:

> See, from his head, his hands, his feet,
> Sorrow and love flow mingled down.
> Did e'er such love and sorrow meet,
> Or thorns compose so rich a crown?[4]

And

> Behold His wounded hands and feet!
> Come touch, and see, and feel,
> The wounds and marks that you may know
> His love for you is real.[5]

Scriptures teach us to open our eyes that we might see, our ears that we might hear, and soften our hearts that we may understand (3 Nephi 11:5). If we do these things, we can have the living water and the bread of life (see John 4:10–14; 6:35). These are very physical acts.

Mortality also allows for emotions. Let's take a closer look at what the Lord teaches Job about our reaction to the plan of salvation: we shouted for joy (see Job 38:7). Did we have joy at that moment? Or perhaps did we shout at the potential joy we could have by coming to earth? Lehi uses that same word—joy—to explain that Adam and Eve fell that we might have joy (see 2 Nephi 2:25). Is joy only attainable by the Fall, the condescension into a mortal, physical world? In mortality, we experience fear, anxiety, discouragement, depression, and a myriad of other emotions. Do we need to feel these in order to understand joy, peace, and hope?

Mortality takes our social relationships to a new dimension. God told Adam that it was not good for him to be alone (see Genesis 2:18). It is not good for any of us to be alone. It is only with our physical bodies that we know the sanctity of marriage, of cleaving to another human being. Again, we become Adam and Eve as we embody this earthly opportunity. We also become Abraham and Sarah, Jacob and Rachel, Hannah and Elkanah, Zacharias and Elizabeth, Joseph and Mary, Joseph and Emma, both in struggles of fertility and in the trouble offspring can bring. The Abrahamic covenant is only realized through the physical experience. Moroni quoted the words of Malachi several times when he visited Joseph Smith, that the hearts of the children would turn to their fathers (see Malachi 4:6; 3 Nephi 25:6; Doctrine and Covenants 2:2; 110:15; Joseph Smith—History 1:39). Joseph expanded the kindred of the house of Israel to include dear friends: "That same sociality which exists among us here will exist among us there, only it will be coupled with eternal glory" (Doctrine and Covenants 130:2). I know in this life I have drawn upon the fasting and prayers of my family and friends to find health and peace, and to find comfort and joy. As Marjorie Hinckley said, "Oh, how we need each other!"[6]

That same mortal sociality, however, would include broken relationships, mortal enemies, and nemeses, even "frenemies." Some of my greatest struggles have been with the people around me. Elder Neal A. Maxwell noted that "we serve as each other's clinical material," meaning that only from interaction with others, sometimes tough and harrowing, allow us the opportunity to repent and forgive, to fill our bowels with compassion and mercy, as Christ did.[7] These too are mortal experiences.

Clinical material is a much nicer phrase than thorns and noxious weeds. There are a couple of reasons why we have broken bodies, broken relationships, and broken promises. Eve realized this after being cast out of the garden: "Were it not for our transgression we never should have had seed, and never should have known good and evil, and the joy of our redemption" (Moses 5:11). There's that word *joy* again. Lehi taught, "It must needs be, that there is an opposition in all things. If not so," he continued, "righteousness could not be brought to pass, neither wickedness, neither holiness, nor misery, neither good nor bad" (2 Nephi 2:11). Mary Fielding Smith learned this same profound truth after leaving the harrowing trials of Missouri, where her husband Hyrum had been imprisoned in Liberty Jail, and she became extremely ill after delivering her first baby. She wrote her brother, Joseph Fielding, in June 1839, "I have, to be sure, been called to drink deep of the bitter cup; but you know, my beloved brother, this makes the sweet sweeter."[8]

The combination or opposition of hard things and good things in mortality equips us with experience. Again, Mary Fielding Smith provides a good example. When Hyrum was in Liberty Jail, communication proved challenging. Letters crossed in the post or were entirely lost, and, as we all know, not hearing from someone we love and are concerned about can cause tenuous friction. Mary wrote to Hyrum, "I believe all our afflictions will work together for our good, altho[ugh] they are not joyous while passing through them."[9] Liberty Jail was certainly a trying experience. When Joseph reached the end of his rope, he pleaded to the Lord: "O God, where art thou? And where is the pavilion that covereth thy hiding

YOUR FAITH HAS MADE YOU WHOLE, BY JORGE COCCO SANTÁNGELO.

place?" (Doctrine and Covenants 121:1–4). Where are you? Why must I experience this separation from you? These verses remind me of what Christ must have felt in the Garden of Gethsemane and on the cross. But Joseph had to experience it for himself. Finally, the Lord responds, "All these things shall give thee experience, and shall be for thy good" (Doctrine and Covenants 122:7). We, like Mary Fielding Smith, or Joseph Smith, even dare I say like Jesus Christ, need that experience to run through us, to break us down, and to allow Christ to fill us up and to heal us from the travesties of mortality and make us whole.

Experience and opposition allow for proof. We prove or proof our bread dough, allowing the yeast to ferment and rise. Some recipes require proofing two times. The plan of salvation required that proof. God said, "We will prove them herewith" (Abraham 3:25). This could mean a trial or proof by a test (see Doctrine and Covenants 98:12). Moroni taught that we would receive no witness until after the trial of our faith (see Ether 12:6, 12). To prove is also to refine—a mortal period of refinement. Laura Clark Phelps stated, "We have to be tried like gold, seven times tried."[10] Since our Heavenly Parents are all-knowing creators, they know who we are. Through experience, I have learned to listen to my body, to recognize its limits and bounds, to push it when necessary, and to provide it with tender repose. Oh, how grateful I am to prove me to myself that I can, indeed, do hard things.[11]

These hard things also prove to me how much I need Christ and his Atonement. I simply cannot do all that mortality requires of me by myself. Mary Fielding Smith became an expert at this recognition. Mary, her sister Mercy, and their brother Joseph left their home and family in England to seek better opportunities in Canada. They found the Church and were baptized there, then moved to Kirtland, where Mercy married her husband and went with him on a mission back to Canada, and Joseph returned to England on a mission. Mary was left alone in Kirtland—no family, no job, and no friends. Maybe Kirtland was one of her desert places. She participated in the charismatic and sacred experiences in the Kirtland Temple, a balm to her lonely soul. And she wrote to her sister, "I feel more and more convinced that it is through suffering that we are to be made perfected." She continued, "I have already found it has the effect of driving one nearer to the Lord and so has become a great blessing to me."[12]

I love the lesson she learned—to allow her suffering not only to refine or prove her, but to draw upon the Lord. We see this unfold throughout the Book of Mormon. At the beginning, Nephi learns that Christ "shall manifest himself unto [those that hearken unto him] in word, and also in power, in very deed, unto the taking away of their stumbling blocks" (1 Nephi 14:1). His younger brother Jacob learned from Nephi, claiming that the Lord shows us our weakness so that we understand the power of his condescension and grace (see Jacob 4:7). Mormon teaches that instead of being upset or judgmental about imperfections, we should "give thanks unto God that he hath made manifest unto you [y]our imperfections, that ye may learn" (Mormon 9:31). Both Mormon and his son Moroni, who had read and edited the accounts of the American inhabitants, realized that a loving, graceful, merciful Savior will actually show us our weakness. If we humble ourselves, with the full recognition of our imperfections, and we turn to Christ and seek His salvific power, our weakness—our thorns in the flesh, our briars and noxious weeds—can be made strong (see Ether 12:26–27; 2 Corinthians 12:9–10). Hallelujah and hosanna—save us now, O Lord.

I came to understand this with my first bone marrow transplant. A successful transplant required the obliteration of my marrow—my immune system—in order to receive new stem cells from my brother. His cells noticed a lack of marrow and worked to build up a new immune system. But in order for that to happen, I came to the brink of death by radiation and intense chemotherapy. I literally felt like a blob of mass.

While receiving my new marrow through a transfusion, I felt myself separating from my body, floating high above my bed in my hospital room. When my nurse slowed the flow and pulled me back into my body, it was just the beginning of my wreck and havoc. My esophagus became so enflamed that I could not eat. I was on IV nutrients and fluids for weeks, as well as a pain pump. Several times I just wove in and out of consciousness, but those IV lines pulled me back down. It was a long journey. My second transplant, from my other brother, happened on Good Friday, 2017. His blood literally saved me.

I have some good news: I have been in remission for four years. That's incredible and not normal for someone whose cancer has recurred four times. The longer I go, the more chance I have of a cure. The other good news is that if or when my DNA shifts again to make leukemia, there are amazing medical advances that could provide me with more time earthside. And if not, I'm going home—home with the big H. How joyous that reunion will be. I can't wait to meet my Savior, my dear friends Jane Snyder Richards and Mary Fielding Smith, my dear grandparents, and so many others.

The good news, the message of Easter is this: we can honor mortality, and we can indeed shout for joy because the Son of God has prepared a more excellent way (Ether 12:11). Physical and emotional experience, along with social connections made along the way, allow us to choose God and be saved. Condescension produces resurrection. Earth has no sorrow that heaven cannot heal.[13] The Lord will remember the covenants I have made, and he will verify his word in every particular (see 1 Nephi 19:15; Alma 25:17). His eternal purposes will roll on (see Mormon 8:22–24). Because of that, I shout for joy.

NOTES

1. Jane Snyder Richards, Reminiscence, 1880, 19–21, Church History Library, Salt Lake City.
2. Priscilla Merriman Evans, Autobiography, [ca. 1907], 42; Emma Priscilla Evans Little, Papers, 1879–1941, L. Tom Perry Special Collections, Harold B. Lee Library, Brigham Young University, Provo, UT; see *The First Fifty Years of Relief Society: Key Documents in Latter-day Saint Women's History*, ed. Jill Mulvay Derr, Carol Cornwall Madsen, Kate Holbrook, and Matthew J. Grow (Salt Lake City: Church Historian's Press, 2016), 221.
3. Melissa Morgan Dodge to William T. Morgan, June 23, 1839, William T. Morgan Correspondence, Church History Library; Ann Marsh Abbott to Nathan Marsh, June 20, 1843, in private possession.
4. Isaac Watts, "Crucifixion to the World by the Death of Christ" ["When I Survey the Wondrous Cross"], *Hymns and Spiritual Songs* (1707).
5. John V. Pearson, "Behold the Wounds in Jesus' Hands" (1998), https://churchofjesuschrist.org/music/library/music-for-choirs?lang=eng.
6. Virginia H. Pearce, ed., *Glimpses into the Life and Heart of Marjorie Pay Hinckley* (Salt Lake City: Deseret Book, 1999), 254.
7. Neal A. Maxwell, "Content with the Things Allotted unto Us," general conference, April 2000; 3 Nephi 17:6–7.
8. Mary Fielding Smith to Joseph Fielding, June 1839, in Edward W. Tullidge, *Women of Mormondom* (New York City: Tullidge and Crandall, 1877), 255–56.
9. Mary Fielding Smith to Hyrum Smith, April 11, 1839, Church History Library.
10. Laura Clark Phelps to John Cooper, 1839, Zula Rich Cole Collection, Church History Library; Psalm 12:6.

11. Elaine Dalton, "A Return to Virtue," general conference, October 2008; "Guardians of Virtue," general conference, April 2011.
12. Mary Fielding Smith to Mercy Fielding Thompson, August–September 1837, Mary Fielding Smith Collection, Church History Library.
13. Thomas Moore, "Come, Ye Disconsolate," *Sacred Songs* (1816).

INDEX

P

R

S